LOVE IN A PANDEMIC

Nichole Humphrey

Copyright © 2020 Nichole Humphrey
All rights reserved.

TABLE OF CONTENTS

Dedication		v
Prologue		vii
Chapter 1	Church On Sunday	1
Chapter 2	The Accident	3
Chapter 3	My New Home	8
Chapter 4	In Sickness And In Health	17
Chapter 5	This Can't Be Real	23
Chapter 6	Recovery	27
Chapter 7	Finally, Home	44
Chapter 8	Healing	49
Chapter 9	Victory	52
Chapter 10	What We Survived	62
Chapter 11	The Interview	65
About The Author		69

DEDICATION

This journaling workbook, along with my personal account of our story is dedicated first to my daughter Alexa Nichole. Alexa, you have challenged me in so many ways and I'm truly grateful that God gifted you to me. I know that you have personally survived your own "Love in a pandemic". You are brave and strong. I thank you for helping me when it has truly counted. I'm excited to see how God maps out the rest of your life. I love you...

To the love of my life, Lance. This book is partly inspired by you. In 2019 We experienced our own "Love in a pandemic". It was your strength, faith, and endurance that got us through. I am forever grateful to God for giving me to you, my soul mate. As a result of the things that we have been through I have been stretched as a person, and I have grown as a wife. I will stand with you through anything. It was an honor to take care of you. We are a true testament that you can survive "Love in a pandemic". I love you...

PROLOGUE

As I began to create this journaling workbook, I started creating the book to help couples maneuver through the current state of the pandemic that we are currently facing today (corona virus). As I began to write I came to the realization that a pandemic is not just the disease for the current season that we are experiencing but, a pandemic can occur when your relationship experiences a crisis situation similar to the crisis that we are currently facing today. It can happen at any given time, and it can happen to any relationship.

Marriages, and relationships face pandemic situations every single day. These pandemic situations can hinder the growth of marriages and relationships. The question on the table is, can you survive? Survival can be difficult, but you can survive! When a pandemic situation is occurring in your relationship, you are often unsure if you have what it takes to survive. Sometimes survival is realized only after you have come out on the other side but being able to make it out is what is important.

Read the true accounts of our "Love in a pandemic" story, from my personal perspective. After which you will be able to journal and utilize tips and tools for how you too can survive "Love in a pandemic".

CHAPTER 1
CHURCH ON SUNDAY

Sunday February 10, 2019. It was a regular Sunday morning except I didn't feel like going to church. There was an agitation in the air on both parts, and it appeared we both didn't want to be bothered. My husband and I got dressed as usual barely speaking words to one another. My ride to the church was loud as I rehearsed music that we would sing that Sunday morning. As usual once we got to church and got the service started, I could feel that both of our attitudes shifted. Church had a way of bringing our spirits together through praise, worship, fellowship, dancing, and of course good preaching. What a powerful word my husband preached that Sunday morning. The church was on fire and everyone was on their feet by the time my husband got to the end of his sermon. My husband had gotten so excited preaching the word, he was standing on the pew. I was so proud and appreciative of the way God showed up in his life each and every Sunday.

Whenever I showed up to the church with an attitude towards him, it was usually gone by the time service was over and vice versa. If I had an attitude on Sunday morning, I was usually in love with him by the time church was over. After church was over per usual, we held the discussion about what we were going to do after church for dinner. I actually drove that Sunday because our daughter had a concert that I was going to attend that Sunday afternoon. We spent time on the church parking lot talking and laughing with other members. This was a normal Sunday ritual. We didn't stay out long because it had begun to snow. It was the pretty, fine, soft snow and it was coming down fast. We decided that we would eat at a restaurant close by our home because of the change in weather. Eating at a place close to home would allow for my husband to go straight home after dinner. He pulled out from the church first and I followed right behind him. This was typical if we were going to the same place but had to drive separate. It was also typical for me to talk on the phone with my husband while I followed behind him. As we were driving on the freeway, we approached a turn. I could hear my husband yelling whoa! I could see that a car had crashed into the side of the freeway. My husband's car began to slide, and my car begin to slide as well. It was very slippery outside due to the falling fine snow. My heart started beating fast because I was afraid an accident would happen. Both of our cars gained traction and we both slowed down.

We finally made it to the restaurant on the eastside of town, about five minutes from our house. Once seated the smiling young man said, may I take your order? My husband asks him, "excuse me do you have chitterlings". The young man said, "I'm so sorry, we are out". Disappointed we both ordered our meals and started to talk about how good service was. The young man quickly returned and said "sir, we had one bowl left and I scraped up all I could for you". My husband was so happy. They brought him the bowl of chitterlings and he ate every bite. He enjoyed them like it was his last time. I said "dang, you didn't even let me get a bite". He said they only gave me a little bit. I told him "you ate those like it was your last time". Little did I know it would be the last time for a while.

CHAPTER 2
THE ACCIDENT

Dinner was over and we paid for our bill. We walked out of the restaurant arm in arm because I slipped and almost fell just as we headed out of the door. We laughed and I told my husband we needed to be careful because this is the kind of snow that will have you broke (meaning, you would fall and hurt yourself). I said to him, "did I tell you I fell on the ground last week at the salon outside". Everyone was watching. I told him one of the stylists (who is a member of our church) came outside to get me up off of the ground. We both started laughing as we headed for our cars. As he got into his car I said, "babe please be careful". He said ok and drove off.

The snow had not let up and it was coming down very fast. It was beautiful, fine, white snow. I was trailing behind my husband, but I veered off to the side of the road to put the traction on my car because my wheels were sliding. I took off just as one of my favorite songs came on the radio. Per usual I turned my radio up as loud as it could go and started to sing at the top of my lungs. I was thankful for how our day had turned out. I was driving about thirty miles per hour being very careful as to not let my car slide (I hate driving in the snow). I was just about two minutes from home when I looked to my left and noticed that a car had been in an accident. The entire front end of the car was totally gone. All I could see was the engine of the wrecked car.

I became very confused trying to figure out if the lady had just crashed. I could see her panicking trying to escape her car. I wasn't sure what was going on with her but, I immediately said to myself out loud "God I hope my husband was not in this accident". Just before I could finish my sentence, I began to notice red skid marks and red car parts in the middle of the road. I slowed way down to see if what I saw was really real. As I began to bring my car to a stop, I could see my husband's car in a ditch. I put my car in park. I jumped out leaving the passenger car door open music still blaring. I ran into the ditch to my husband's car. The entire left side of his car was completely smashed in and the front windshield was split down the middle. I yelled Lance! What happened! He looked at me and said, "Nichole she just hit me". He turned his head and faded out for a few seconds.

I began screaming at the top of my lungs LANCE!!!!!!!! I was frantic. I ran into the middle of the street yelling and screaming "somebody help me"! For about five seconds it was as if time stood still. No one was on the road but me, my husband and the lady who hit him head on. I remembered grabbing my phone when I jumped out of the car and with shaking, trembling hands I dialed 911. By this time, it was lightly snowing but freezing cold and I felt nothing but anguish. "911 may I help you", the lady asked. All I could do was scream at the top of my lungs and cry PLEASE CAN YOU HELP ME! "Mam, please try and calm down, what is your name"? Um…. Um… I don't know (crying). I could not recall my name at that time. I screamed, "Lady please help me"! What is your name? She asked again. "Nikki my name is Nikki and this lady hit my husband!" "Where are you?" "Um…. Um…. I'm on, I don't know"! "Please lady, please help me"! I was so distraught I couldn't even tell her where I was. I literally blanked out. I couldn't even give the street even though it was only two minutes from my home. Ok she said, what happen? I told her as best as I could, this lady hit my husband in his car. She asked, is he conscious"? I said I don't know. She asked me if he was breathing and I completely lost it. The thought of him not breathing would have killed me. They finally said, "mam we found you". I immediately heard sirens although they seemed miles away. I ran back to my husband's crushed vehicle. I thought to myself she got out of her car, why is he still in the car. I soon realized that he could not get out of his car on his own.

Right before the squad pulled up an African gentleman appeared and got into the ditch with my husband. He put his hand through the window and placed it on my husband's chest. He began to pray and speak in tongues over my husband. Not only did he stop to offer prayer and comfort, but a young lady and her daughter stopped to comfort me and tell me everything would be alright. The lady who hit my husband appeared to be fine. She held me and we cried. She just kept saying "I'm sorry, I'm sorry". I was so hysterical that she started praying and dropped to her knees. I actually thought she passed out, and I was thinking not you to. Once the emergency squad and police arrived, I thought they would help my husband get out of his car. There was one big problem, he couldn't get out of his car because his left leg was mashed in with the car door. The paramedics ask me to stand back away from the car and at first, I refused. I wanted to see everything that was getting ready to happen to my husband. The police officer and the African man convinced me that I had to stand back in order for them to help get my husband out of his car. They took out an object that looked like a large pair of metal scissors, it was huge (jaws of life). They began to cut the door of the car in order for my husband to be freed from the vehicle. More tears began to fall from my eyes, and I felt like I was having a panic attack while I was watching.

I couldn't believe this was happening. I couldn't believe I found the accident and I couldn't believe I called 911. I kept screaming "something is wrong with his legs", and I was crying uncontrollably. Every time I said something was wrong with his legs, the African man would say, using his accent "calm down they can fix them". The way he said it makes me and my aunt laugh even to this today. I was a complete mess. The African man and police officer truly tried to calm me, but no one could calm me down I was to hysterical. My whole life was flashing before my eyes. My husband was helpless and there was nothing I could do for him. I could do absolutely nothing! It was painful to see him go through this, and my heart was being crushed as I watched him go through this. As they pulled my husband out of his crushed vehicle and placed him on the stretcher he moaned. I could tell he was in pain, but he didn't want to alarm me, so he didn't yell. My eyes zeroed in on his legs and I could tell that both of his legs were broken. As he laid on the stretcher his legs appeared mangled as if a dog had eaten them up. Through my tears the last words I spoke to my husband at that time was "don't worry ok, everything will be ok". I stated this as tears rolled down my face not truly knowing if things would be ok. As the paramedics put my husband in the emergency squad the first person, I called was my mom. I could barely get any words out. All I could do was cry with agony, MOM!!!! I finally was calm enough to tell her what was going on. She told me to be calm and everything would be ok. She told me to stay put and she would come and get me. I told her to meet me at the hospital because I was driving there. She said, no, my brother or sister would come and get me because I didn't need to drive. I told her not to come because I was leaving so we hung up the phone.

My phone immediately began ringing. The first call was my sister, and I could tell she was upset but didn't want to make me more upset because I answered the phone crying. "Nikki, where are you"? I told her where I was, and she asked me to stay there. I told her "NO! I'm leaving." My phone started to beep, and it was my brother. "Sis, what is going on? I'm right around the corner, I'm on my way." I told him to meet me at the hospital because I was on my way there. First my sister, "where are you I'm coming". Then my brother "I'm right around the corner sis, where are you, I'm coming". I was hysterical and screaming, "NO! I'm driving behind the squad!" I wanted to be close to my husband and make sure nothing else happened to him. I was in a state of shock. I cried so hard at the thought of having to call his mom with this news, but I finally made the call. My reaction with her was the same reaction I had when I called my mom. I could barely get the words out. She listened to me very intently and very calmly. I told her where they were taking him, and we ended our call. My last and final call was to our daughter. I knew this would not be good, so I called my sister to go and find her at the mall where she was looking for a shirt for her concert. Once she answered the phone I stayed as calm as I possibly could. I tried to pretend that I was not hysterically crying. With a quivering voice I gave her the news and right there in the mall she lost it. It hurt me so bad that I could not hold her in the moment.

I had to tell her then because I didn't want her to find out from anyone else. I tried my best to not make it sound as bad as it looked. I told her that her aunt was on her way to the mall to pick her up and to just wait there and not drive. The squad pulled off with my whole life on the inside of it. I slowly climbed back into my car with the music still blaring not even remembering I had been listening to a song. The officers had cleared my husband's car parts from out of the road so that I could get by. I turned the radio completely off. I actually had to drive right by our house because of the wreckage. I didn't stop as I wanted to get to the hospital as quick as I could. I prayed all the way to the hospital. My crying prayer went something like this: God, I don't understand what just happened but whatever you do PLEASE DON'T LET MY HUSBAND DIE!

CHAPTER 3

MY NEW HOME

When I arrived at the hospital most of my family was there waiting on me. I initially put on my strong brave face suggesting that I was fine (I WASN'T)! I pulled my mom off to the side and told her "Mom I think both of his legs are broken". She looked at me as if I was unsure. I described how the legs looked and she just assured me that we would be ok. It seemed like a lifetime of waiting to get word regarding if my husband had arrived. While I waited to hear information on my husband, I called four of his best friends. They were all very upset when I shared with them what happened to their friend. One of his friends, who is a pastor in the city was there in a matter of minutes after I had called him. He walked in the waiting area where my family was seated and dropped to his knees in front of a window and prayed. After he prayed, he got up and hugged me and we cried. He stayed for about ten minutes comforting our family and then he left. Finally, a social worker came and said, "we have five doctors working on him". I began to cry because what did that mean. Was he dying? Were they trying to save him? What was going on? I kept telling myself, ok he broke both his legs. They will put him into two cast and send him home. He will be mad about being into two cast but, we would manage. (if you know my husband you would understand that statement). After about two hours the social worker called, Humphrey!

My daughter and I jumped up and ran to meet her. She said you can see him now. We slowly walked through several doors and finally made it to a back room where they were holding my husband. We didn't know what to expect. We cried as we got closer not knowing what we would fine. When we walked into his room, we could tell he was glad to see us. He was lying in a neck brace and we could tell that he was in a lot of severe pain. I held one hand and Alexa held the other hand. He asks us if we were ok. Of course, I lied and said we are fine, but I was shaking on the inside. We stood there in silence holding hands. I mostly kept repeating silent prayers, help us God. We still had no answers and God was the only one who could help us. A nurse came in and shared with us that there had been about nineteen accidents due to the unexpected weather. A doctor finally showed up and shared with us all of the injuries that my husband had suffered. He also told us that my husband would have to have emergency surgery in order to save his legs, especially the right one. Not even thinking I asked, "will he go home tonight?" The doctor informed me that he would not be going home tonight. I thought to myself, ok surgery tomorrow and then home. My daughter and I kissed my husband and left the room so that his sister could come in and see him. Alexa and I walked to the waiting area where our family was being held and I gave them the update that was shared with us.

They moved all of our family and friends to the surgery waiting area. They allowed me to wait upstairs with my husband until they were ready to take him to surgery. The area that they placed us in was cold, and quiet. In the pre-surgery room it was me, my husband and the nurse who would take him back to surgery when the doctor was ready for him. He would be having emergency surgery on his right leg in order for them to save it. We sat in that room at times in silence, but me mostly praying. We held hands and told each other how much we loved one another. Nothing else mattered in that moment. Nothing he had done, nothing I had done. Stupid arguments over the kitchen, nothing! I was nervous for what was to come but I remained calm because he was calm. I was ok because he was ok. A doctor entered the room who I now know was the orthopedic surgeon. He explained that a fixator would have to be placed on my husband's right leg in order to basically save it. The fixator would hold his leg together until they could figure out how to rebuild it. We agreed to allow the doctor to do whatever he could to save the leg and fix whatever was wrong. We were also told that Lance's right foot would have to be rebuilt because it had been completely crushed as a result of the accident. He suffered a broken fibula and a broken tabula in his right leg. The bone in his leg had come through his flesh and this was just the beginning. The nurse walked into the room and said the doctor was ready for Lance. I prayed for him one last time, kissed him gently on the lips, and told him I loved him. I also told the nurse to tell the doctor to be extra careful with him. She said she would relay the message.

Once I arrived back in the family waiting area I was greeted with hugs and more questions. Family ask, how is he? How is his spirit? How are you? I just said ok because I had no real answers to those questions. I just wanted to be home with my husband. While we waited, we started watching and award show and all I wanted to see was the hot new female rapper. Watching her perform for those few minutes made me feel like I was at home and it was a great escape from my new reality. Once her performance was over everything went back to normal. Surgery ended around one a.m. or so. The doctor stated everything went well but there would be a lot of pain. They also informed me he would be going to trauma ICU. I ask how long will we be here? The doctor informed me that it would be at least two weeks before they would even entertain him going home. I heard what the doctor said but I don't think it registered. Just as the doctor was walking away my husband's brother in-love ask the doctor if my husband would be able to go on our 25th wedding anniversary cruise to Spain. We had been anticipating this trip and we were going to go with two other couples. The doctor told him, we need to cancel those plans and we should probably cancel any other plans we had for the rest of the year.

He told us that there was a strong chance that my husband would not be able to walk without assistance in June. This is when we were scheduled to take our trip. I thought to myself wow; we have to cancel Spain. It was only February and I couldn't see past that night. I told my family and our friends they should go home after seeing my husband because they had been there just about all night long. I knew they were tired. Just about everyone had left the hospital and went home after we were settled in our new home (trauma ICU). I walked into my husband's room and found him lying there in an extreme amount of pain. It was heart breaking. My husband was all wrapped up in blankets from head to toe. The first thing I did was pull the cover back from his right leg because I could see huge steal, rods coming from up out of the blanket. I did not expect to see what I saw. His leg was literally being held together by large steel rods. I had never seen anything like it in my whole life. It literally looked like a scene from Jesus being nailed to the cross. It was three steel rods. One held the thigh together, one held the knee together, and the other held his ankle together. The three steel rods were implanted into his leg. It was unreal to see his leg like that. His leg was black, swollen, and three times the size. I described to my husband what I saw but, it was too difficult for him to see it, so he didn't look. I knew he was tired, and I wanted him to rest, I was tired, and I needed rest. We both agreed I should go home and come back in the morning.

I went home early Monday morning around three a.m. When I walked into our home without my husband I fell on the floor and cried. The longest we had spent nights apart was four days when he would take a trip for his birthday. Before I left the hospital, I was given a bag with all of my husband's personal belongings. It was most of the items he had with him from Sunday. I knew that it didn't matter if I had gone through the bag now or later it would be emotional for me. I decided to do it and get it over with. I opened up the bag and found bloody boots, jeans, and the shirt he had on. I could tell they had to cut him out of his clothes because most of the items were shredded. I cried as I pulled the items out of the bag one by one. This was horrible. Once I separated items that I would keep and items I would throw away I took them to the trash can outside. I managed to sleep about three hours before I woke up and remembered what happened. As soon as I opened my eyes I started crying. I cried in the shower. I cried getting dressed and I cried all the way back to the hospital. When I arrived, my husband was in so much pain but nevertheless he was alive, and we were glad to see each other. Monday was a hard day. I walked into the room and tried to be strong, but I lost it. I started crying and once I started crying my husband started crying. He thought I was withholding information regarding his injuries. He thought he was paralyzed, and I was keeping it from him. I was just so sad he was in this state. We calmed ourselves and for the rest of the day I was meeting all the doctors on his case, getting use to the nurses and the hospital routine. I spent a lot of time on the phone with my job and cancelling our cruise. I also had to make the dreadful call to a university that I was enrolled in. I explained to the lady that I would have to drop out of the doctoral program because I had to take care of my husband. The day was full of doctors, and nurses, coming in and out of the room making Lance share his story over and over again.

Word had gotten around the city about the horrible tragedy that had taken place with Lance and the hospital waiting area was full the next day. I spent all day by his side, asking questions, holding his hand and of course crying. At times we just cried together. We couldn't believe this was happening. All day Monday my husband struggled to rest due to the pain. I prayed for him to get some sleep. We all prayed for him to get some sleep. Lance became concerned because he had left his briefcase, the church keys, and some other personal items in his car. Along with everything else I spent all day Monday trying to track down which tow company had his car. I finally found the tow company and agreed I would go there as soon as they opened Tuesday morning. I got up and got dressed early Tuesday morning. It was pitch black outside and freezing cold. The tow company didn't open until seven, so I parked my car outside the lot and began to wait. I noticed a lot of traffic inside the building, so I got out of the car and went in. The man immediately told me they were not open. My eyes filled with tears and I said "sir can you please let me get my husband's items out of his car. I needed to get back to the hospital. I shared what happened and the gentleman was nice enough to let me come in at six thirty. He had me sign some papers and explained the cars are held down the street. I ask are you going with me? He said "mam, you have to go there by yourself". I got back into my car and drove a mile down the road and pulled into a lot where a bunch of cars had been damaged. I drove until I spotted my husband's car. I pulled right in front of it. I started crying and I also became physical sick just looking at his car and the damage that had been done. I pulled myself together and talked myself through getting out and climbing into his vehicle. Climbing into the car was my only way of getting into it. It seemed to have been smashed together. I could see his bag, but it was not easily accessible. I had to pull back the windshield which was now in the back seat. The keys were lodged in the ignition and there was no way to retrieve them. I finally managed to get all of the needed items out of the car. Right before I was getting ready to make my exit, I found my husband's eyeglasses lying on the floor up front on the passenger's side. I was so grateful for finding those he needed those because he needed them. I left grateful to have finally gotten out of there. It was hard to see the car in that condition. I arrived back at the hospital and found my husband asleep and I was grateful for that. He had literally slept all day Tuesday and we were all thanking God for that.

That night our church held a citywide prayer meeting for my husband. My first thought was not to attend because I didn't want to answer any questions that I didn't have the answers to. I ended up attending with my sisters and I'm glad I did. I arrived at the church a little late because my husband was expecting a visitor. The mayor of our city asked if he could please come and see my husband. We thought it was an honor for the mayor to come and visit him due to his busy schedule. The mayor and my husband had become really good acquaintances. I allowed the mayor and the attorney general to come and see my husband because I knew seeing them would lift his spirit. Not only did he get a visit from them he got a call from a D.C congress woman. This meant the world to my husband and it lifted his spirit. I was willing to do anything to put him in good spirits. I was so grateful that I attended the service because that service lifted my spirit much. I felt better, I felt decent, I felt like we could make it. Tuesday night was still a very restless night for my husband. Wednesday morning came and Lance seem to be doing pretty good. I was optimistic and I felt like he was to. We both managed to talk without crying and we even smiled a little that morning. A doctor who is a member of our church also worked at the hospital. She surprised us and ordered us a meal from a local food truck. Lance had not had an appetite for the last few days but wanted to try this delicious white bean chili soup that she had bought. I told him how good it was and asked if he wanted some. He said "yes, I will try it". For some strange reason I ask him if he wanted me to feed him. To my surprise he said yes. I thought that was strange, but I paid no attention to it because I was willing to do anything I could in order for him to be comfortable. As I was feeding him the soup, I noticed that when I would place the spoon in his mouth his face would shift to the side. It gave me an eerie feeling because it reminded me of someone having a stroke. I paid no attention to it because he was enjoying his soup and for the first time he appeared to not be in any pain.

For the first time since being in the hospital I was able to visit with family and friends in the family waiting area. That afternoon I was able to share tears and laughs with my family and friends. I even managed to eat a little bit. In January I had started a keto diet and for the first time I was doing really good and losing weight. I actually had kept up with the diet, even with everything that I had going on. One of my good friends who's a drummer came to see me and offered me ice cream with a Reese cup. I asked him, "should we really get a Reese cup with the ice cream". He answered, "there is no other way to eat this ice cream". I thought to myself, how could I turn down this newfound treat and he had a good point. So, with that being said, keto was over for me and I haven't done it since. Around six o'clock p.m. my aunt came rushing down the hall to get me. She had a look of worry on her face and she began to tell me that Lance was trying to get out of the bed and said he was leaving the hospital. She said something wasn't right. I thought to myself ok, no worries, I will get him together. When I walked into his room, he started to question why he was there, and said he wanted to go home. I tried to explain to him that he could not walk, and he could not go home. The more I tried to explain this to him the more upset he became. He started telling me I was allowing people to hold him against his will on the roof of the hospital. I was in such shock I started to laugh nervously. I kept asking him did he trust me, and he answered yes. I told him "you know I wouldn't let anyone harm you and keep you against your will". Lance became very irate because for some reason he did not believe me. His nurse finally entered the room and once she did Lance became very quiet. He only spoke long enough to tell the nurse I was letting people hold him against his will. I told the nurse to call the doctor because something was not right. My husband had become angry to the point that he started to rip out his iv and come out of his clothes. He kept telling me he was getting out of the bed to leave. He was trying to escape and threats of strapping him down did not matter. "Lance"! I yelled, "if you don't calm down, they are going to strap you to this bed, and you will be mad". He answered back "let them try it". He gave me the evilest look he could give me. His nurse told me, "he probably has delirium". I said what is that? She explained it's something patients get after being in the hospital when they have been in to long. I said, he has that after only being in the hospital for three days. She told me to quickly open the blinds so that day light could be in his room. I quickly lifted all the blinds and ask Lance where he was. He just kept saying you know where I am, I'm on the roof. I was thinking JESUS! Please help me! At this point I didn't know what to believe all I knew was that on top of everything else he was now losing his mind.

CHAPTER 4

IN SICKNESS AND IN HEALTH

One of the nurses from another unit came into the room to ask what was going on. I explained to her what his duty nurse told me about the delirium. She got a strange look on her face, hmm, she said. By this time several doctors and nurses were in the room all trying to figure out what was going on. I had called in all the doctors and nurses who could help me. The nurse who had come in his room to see what was going on whispered in my ear and said ask for a CAT scan. She said, tell them to give him a scan to see if something is going on. I immediately started to demand they give him a CAT scan. I called my mom and told her something is not right. In order to calm me they agreed to give him a CAT scan. As they rolled him away if looks could kill, I would be dead. He was so angry with me for letting people hold him against his will, but I could not convince him that it wasn't true. When he left the room the duty nurse came in to convince me that he had delirium and it could last up to six weeks. She shared with me one of her other patients had it and tried to beat her up. I told her; I can't go through this for six weeks because he's mad at me for this. The scan literally took about thirty minutes. I was called back into the room but this time about four doctors walked in and they were all neurologist. I thought nothing of it because they always came into our room in teams. I assumed they were coming to tell me he had delirium. The female doctor took out a sheet of paper that appeared to be some sort of report. She said Mrs. Humphrey we did the CT scan, and this is what the report showed. Your husband has suffered three strokes. All I heard were strokes. I fell to the floor screaming and crying Jesus, why? God please help me! Why is this happening? I had reached a total breaking point and right then and there I was having a break down. I found myself on the floor in the hospital hallway screaming and crying. I had had enough! Half of the doctors stayed in the room and the other half came into the hallway to check on me. Mrs. Humphrey are you ok? No! I'm not ok, I knew something was wrong with him. Why is this happening! I cried. They immediately called for the Chaplin, not for my husband but for me. My mom in-love and my mom showed up in a matter of seconds to try and calm me. I was distraught, I was tired, I was defeated, I was hurt, and I was still confused as to why this was happening. I was truly in a pandemic situation. I calmed myself long enough to speak to the neurologist by video chat. They were trying to decide if we had to move to another hospital because of the strokes he endured. At this point they were trying to figure out what was important the state of his legs or the strokes. It was decided that he would stay at the hospital that we were currently in. This decision was decided because there was nothing that they could do regarding the strokes at all.

We were told that a blood clot traveled to a hole in his heart that we didn't even know existed. The blood clot lodged on the left side of his brain causing three strokes. They told me the window of opportunity to try and do something about it was an hour after it happened. I immediately began to beat myself up. I thought if only, I would have said something about his mouth when I saw it, I could have helped the situation. Till this day I feel guilty about that. I finally calmed down and accepted that we had to face another battle, although difficult I told myself we could survive this to. My husband seemed much calmer and I ask him if he understood what was going on. He said yes and ask to hold my hand. I ask if he thought I was letting people hold him hostage. He said no because the way he heard me cry. He said he knew that I was not holding him hostage. That night I officially moved into the hospital vowing to not leave his side as long as he was in there. For the next seventeen days I lived at the hospital with my husband. I made a quick trip to a local store and bought a ten dollar blow up bed, sheets and extra blankets so I could try and make it as comfortable as I could. The hospital was kind enough to give me a day pass so that I could shower there daily. One of my aunts gave me the keys to her apartment so that I could shower there as well. She lived not too far from the hospital. I never took her up on the offer because although I didn't like it, it was easier for me to just do it at the hospital, so I didn't have to leave. Every morning I would wake up and take a ten-minute walk to the other side of the hospital. I showered amongst strangers, using hospital towels, and wash clothes to clean myself each day. The first day was the worst. I have the nerve to have OCD (LOL) so to touch anything that was not mine made me sick. After about the fourth day I settled into my new home and I had gotten comfortable with this new way of life. The gentleman who let me in every morning became my buddy offering me free snacks they had available for the doctors and nurses. I never had to worry about eating while I was at the hospital. My sister organized a system for people to bring food to us every single day. I never had to worry about food or eating whether I ate it or not.

The same week that my husband had suffered three strokes he was due to have surgery that same week. It was time to remove the fixator that held his right leg together. We anticipated the removal because it was torture for him to have it on. After enduring the strokes Lance's orthopedic surgeon made the decision to cancel the surgery that was scheduled for that Friday. He shared with us that he made the decision to cancel however he needed to meet with us on Friday. He wanted to discuss our options moving forward. Friday came and it was time for the meeting. The surgeon entered the room with one of his partners to discuss how we should possibly move forward due to the new medical findings. The more they spoke the more my heart raced and sank at the same time. I tried my best to hold back the tears as they shared with us the news that my husband would have a fifty percent chance of coming through the surgery, walking, or possibly living. They explained to us that if he didn't have the fixator removed within the next few days, he would have to leave it on for the next eight weeks. If we made this decision his leg would grow with the fixator. Once the fixator was finally removed after the eight weeks, they told us he would not be able to walk on that leg again. The other option was to have the surgery and allow them to remove the fixator, but the downside would be a major stroke and they were very clear that another stroke would be fatal. I told the doctors I could not decide, I didn't know what to do. I ask both of the doctors, what would they do if it was their family member. One doctor said that if it were his family, he would not have the surgery and take the chance of not walking but at least there would be life.

 The other doctor said he would go through with the surgery and take a chance. How could I take a chance with the love of my life? The father of my child, and my pastor. This was too much for me to bear. My sister in-love along with the doctors left out of the room. They wanted us to take some time to think about our decision. I held my husband's hand and we both cried. He said Nichole, I trust God. I'm going to have the surgery. I was so afraid, but I believed my husband heard from God. We called our family and close friends into the room and shared Lance would be having surgery on Monday. What we did not share with everyone was the odds the doctors had given us. As a family we decided to pray, and God knows I needed all of the prayer I could get. This prayer time was very emotional for so many reasons. I had a thousand things running through my head thinking about what the doctors had said. I had also told Alexa and I was worried about her emotional state as well. Right before the prayer went forth, we began to cry. It was a very emotional, sad, confusing time for our family. I wanted my husband to walk and I didn't want him to die. My mother in-love and my daughter had the toughest time during the prayer. My daughter became hysterical and had a panic attack right there in the hospital room. My mother in-love slumped over in a chair in the room. We were a total mess. As our daughter's hyperventilation began to worsen my husband called our daughter over to his bedside. He laid hands on her and calmed her spirit. I thought what an amazing man. With everything that he was going through he was still a father and a pastor. We prayed, cried, and pulled ourselves together. This had become routine especially since it seemed as though all hell would break loose every other day. Everyone cleared the room except for me of course. Once we were alone, I told my husband "when the doctors come in, I'm going to anoint them and pray". He said, "Nichole they may not want you to pray". He said, "can you just put the oil on your hands and when you touch them, say a silent prayer and they won't know". I said, "bet I don't, when they come in here, they are getting prayed for". I did not have time for any games because we had already been through so much. The doctors returned and ask what our decision was. My husband told them his decision was to move forward with the surgery and they agreed to operate. Before they walked out of his room I said, "excuse me". Are you both going to be doing the surgery?" They answered yes. I said, "do you mind if I pray and ask God to bless us all?" They joyfully answered, "not at all, we need all the prayer we can get for this." I prayed that God would bless them and anoint their hands and to give them strength. We all agreed and received God's blessing for the surgery.

Monday which was surgery day finally came and the family waiting room was packed. We had literally taken it over. We were very polite to other families who were there, offering them food and beverages. We were not the only family suffering. The room was filled with family, friends, and some of our church members from our church. I didn't want to go to the waiting room right away, so I went and found the hospital chapel. As I went into the Chapel, I found a worker sitting on his phone talking as loud as he could. I stopped, paused, and turned around because it appeared, he was not leaving anytime soon. As I closed the door, I rolled my eyes thinking, I can't even pray in peace. I prayed to myself as I walked to the family waiting area. I was so nervous. All I could think about was the doctor who told us he shouldn't have the surgery. When I got to the waiting room everyone was talking, laughing and eating.

I sat with earphones in my ear listening to gospel music, trying to image I was someone else. Surgery took a long time because not only did they have to remove the fixator, but they had to rebuild his right foot. Humphrey, the doctor yelled out. I ran over to the doctor who was already talking to my sister in-love. She was a nurse who understood just about everything that was going on. She was a huge help medically. The doctor explained that everything went really well, and the fixator had been removed and they were able to rebuild the ankle that had been completely crushed. He did not have a stroke on the table. He was still here with us. I shared the news with everyone in the room. Everyone cheered, clapped and thanked God. I did share those sentiments and I told God thank you however, I didn't feel like I could celebrate just yet. I felt in my spirit something else was brewing and I just couldn't get settled.

CHAPTER 5
THIS CAN'T BE REAL

After my husband came out of recovery, I asked one question, "is he in his right mind". They told me he in his right mind however, he had some weird conversation about being in Florida, but he was ok. We settled back into his room and by this time most of our family and friends had left the hospital. After a while, it was just the two of us again. The surgeon that recommended that we didn't go through with the surgery burst into the room around ten-thirty p.m. "Lance! I can't believe it, you made it" he said! Those were the doctor's exact words. He said "I was really worried about you and didn't think you would survive without having a stroke. He said "Lance! I want you to know that you are a miracle." My husband and I were very excited to hear what the doctor shared. I thought it was pretty awesome for the doctor to acknowledge that Lance was a miracle. We both felt good considering everything that had transpired. For the first time Lance and I both felt some relief. The next morning the main orthopedic surgeon came into the room and he was also excited to see my husband. He said, "Lance, you are a miracle". He shared with us that for the first time ever he was able to attach the ankle to a chain in order to hold things in place. He told us he had never been able to do that before. He said, "that prayer truly worked". I told him "God answers prayer". Lance and I both were really pleased with what the doctor had told us. I began making calls sharing the good news with our family and friends. I felt really good and at that point I felt like we could start recovery. We had a good morning and an even better day. Lance was in pain but, it was something he was learning to live with. Lance had stayed up all day so that he could sleep at night (something that was a major struggle for him). It was around ten p.m. and he was dozing off. It appeared he was getting ready to have a good night's rest but then the nurse came into the room and asked, "Lance, did you want your sleeping medicine?" Everything within me said he doesn't need it because he was almost sleep. I told him I didn't think he needed it, but he could make the choice. He told her he wanted it because he was told it would help him sleep.

The nurse gave him the sleeping medicine and he dozed off to sleep. I was extremely tired, so I got in my blow-up bed right next to the hospital bed and I fell asleep fast. I was thinking this was going to be a great night because we could finally sleep. A few hours later I heard a nurse say, "Lance, honey what are you doing?" She had been watching his monitor and could tell he was moving. I sat up to find him out of his hospital gown, with all of the tubes ripped from his chest. Not only that, he had managed to rip the IV right out of his arm and blood was everywhere. I thought to myself, not again. I did not want to relive that first episode. As calm as I could, I said "Lance, where are you going?" He immediately started with "how dare you let them do this to me!" My eyes widened, I said, "do what"? He said, "you know what I'm talking about"? I said, "Lance what is your birthday", and he angrily quoted all of the information, full name, birthday. He also told me what hospital he was at. This assessment was done every time a doctor or nurse came into his room. They were always assessing his cognitive skills, as a result of the stroke. I said, where are you? He said, "you had them take me to a room on the top floor and you're letting them hold me here"! I said to myself Jesus please help me. I was tired and it was around two a.m. and he was starting this foolishness. I said, "Lance you are in the same room and we did not move you". He said, "yes you did, you took me out of the room and now you have me on the top floor". The more I tried to convince him that he had not been moved the more upset he became. I begged and pleaded for him to calm down. He said, "I'm leaving"! I explained that he had to stay in bed because both of his legs are broke. He said, "no they are not, and you are letting them do this to me"! I kept saying you know I would not let anyone harm you and you can't leave because of your legs. I started to look for the call button, but he had it in his hands. I knew this was really bad because he was yelling and blaming me for him being in a place that he was not in. Tears welled up in my eyes and I said, "Lance please stop this"! He said, "if you don't let me out of here, I'm going to hit you"! He said, "this is all your fault" as he began ripping medical tape from off his chest. I tried softly calling for the nurse, I didn't want to alarm the other patients. That didn't work because no one came. I called out again and still no one came. Lance was getting angrier and angrier and the man in front of me was not my husband. I didn't know who this was. He kept saying "I'm leaving"! I became so frustrated I said, "go ahead, get out the bed and leave"! He said, "I CAN'T"! I told him; "I know you can't remember your legs are broke". He said, "you think this is funny don't you". "You think it's a game". "He said if you don't let me leave, I'm going to hit you"! I said "Lance Humphrey, you better not hit me"! Before I could get the last words out, he picked up the hospital remote, swung it around to get some force and he hit me. I couldn't believe it! I was in total shock, he just hit me! He really hit me! He wasn't done either. He also picked up a used urinal and through it at me but, I was able to dodge that. I said, "if you are going to be violent towards me, I'm leaving"! I was crying by this time and he did not care about my tears. For the first time ever, I became afraid of my husband and I was alone. I didn't want to leave him in the room by himself, and it hurt me to do it, but I had no choice.

I ran out the room and started yelling for the nurse. It was at least another 3-4 minutes before she came down the hall. Once we got back to the room, we couldn't believe what we saw. The room was a complete mess. Lance had torn up the entire room from his hospital bed. We were both shocked. I had never seen this behavior before and neither had the nurse. She said "Nichole, he's such a nice guy and not this person". By this time, I was mad, sad, and still in disbelief. Water was everywhere and he had thrown everything he could get his hands on to the floor. He was completely out of his hospital gown and he was still looking at the both of us like we had wronged him in some way. To make matters worse that IV had to go back into his arm and it was a struggle to get that one in. The nurse and I waited until the phlebotomist showed up to try and put his IV back in his arm. She arrived about thirty minutes later and started on the right arm. There was no luck with that arm, so she moved on to the left arm. I could tell he was still mad as she worked on putting the IV in. I could see him rolling his eyes at her and all I kept praying was Lord please don't let him bash this sweet woman in her head. Because of all of the poking that he had previously gone through finding a vein was difficult and it took at least thirty minutes for the top phlebotomist to get his IV in his arm. She finally finished and it was around four a.m. when he finally settled down. I sat up in my blow-up bed the entire night watching, listening, and praying that he didn't have any more episodes. It was around six a.m. and like clockwork my sister in-love called me to see how his night was. I snuck out of the room into the hallway whispering so I didn't wake him up and simply said it was not good and I need you to come here right now because I'm leaving. I was pissed! I was tired, sleepy, and had been up all night. My mind was racing. Would this keep happening? What about when we go home? I was afraid and mad at the same time. Not really mad at him but just at everything. My sister in-love arrived shortly after our phone call. As soon as she walked into the room, I said bye, and I don't know when I'm coming back!

CHAPTER 6

RECOVERY

I walked into our home, a place that now seemed so foreign to me. It was always difficult to come home especially because I knew my husband would not be coming home with me anytime soon. I told myself snap out of it. The goal was to lay down, wake up and shower in my own bathroom for a change. I would also get some fresh clothes and get back to the hospital. I got into our bed around seven a.m. and although it was difficult (tossing and turning) I eventually fell asleep and woke up around one o'clock in the afternoon. I woke up to a ton of missed calls and text messages as usually. I only returned the call of our daughter because she wanted an update. I explained to her everything that had gone on with her dad the night before. She couldn't believe he acted that way, but she was more upset about the sleeping medicine they kept pumping him with. As soon as she got to the hospital that day, she found the nurse on duty and said put in my dad's record that he is to get no more of that medicine. She had looked it up and saw where it caused patients to hallucinate. Another family also told us that the same thing happened to their love one the night before. We decided that he would not receive any more sleep aids as long as he was there. Alexa and my sister in-love were at the hospital so, I felt more comfortable taking my time. I couldn't stand not being at the hospital with my husband and my anxiety started to rise because I was not there. I begin to hurry and get dressed. My daughter called and said as soon as her dad woke up, he started to look for me. She told him I was gone, and he better hope I come back because he acted up. He had no idea what she was talking about. He remembered nothing about the night before until I showed him the pictures I took of the evidence. I arrived back at the hospital about an hour later. I was so excited to see my husband. He was laying there watching TV and he had managed to eat something.

Lance was calm and was resting for most of the day. He hadn't had any of his crazy episodes. Things appeared to be going well, and I felt like the worse was over and we were headed towards recovery. His surgeon came in a few hours later and said, Lance I got your MRI report results for your left knee. I'm sorry to tell you guys this but you are going to have to go back to surgery. By this time, I think I was immune to it because all I said was ok. As he read the report, he told us all the ligaments had been torn around the knee and his hamstring had been completely ripped from the bone. They would have to do a meniscus repair as well as an ACL repair. We were now looking at surgery number three. He would have to be put to sleep once again and this concerned both of us. I ask the doctor when the surgery would take place. "This Friday", the surgeon answered. Once again, we prepared to go back into surgery.

I had been keeping my Gran Gran informed of everything that was going on with Lance. She loved Lance very much and was proud that I was doing so good with my life here in Ohio (she lived in Bastrop, Texas). We connected only three years ago, and it was the best three years of both of our lives. She was my father's mother and for most of my adult life I didn't know she existed. As an adult

I found out that my father had been adopted. He introduced me to his biological mother a few years after his adopted mom passed away. The connection we had to one another was instant after I reached out to her three years ago. I had traveled to Texas several times to visit her and her dogs. Lance and Alexa had traveled to Texas with me as well. She loved that she had a great gran daughter and that is what she called Alexa, her great gran. She would call me and say how is my great gran doing. I loved her and she loved me. I learned so much from her in three years. I also learned that I was a lot like her. She was spunky, feisty, opinionated, and loved to have a good time. Yep, that's exactly who I am.

It was time for surgery and Lance's doctors gave me permission to walk with them to the surgery area. I walked with the doctor's as the wheeled Lance over to the surgery room. They allowed me sit with him unit it was time to go back to surgery. As I was sitting with Lance my phone rang, it was my Gran Gran's Mexican neighborhood. He said I needed to talk to her because she didn't feel well and refused to go to the hospital. I said, "put her on the phone". Once she got on the phone, I immediately updated her with what was going on with Lance. She always asked about him even before the accident. I started in with my usual speech to her about going to the hospital. I said, Gran Gran, please go to the hospital if you don't feel well. She said, NO! I'm not going anywhere! She was adamant about not going to the hospital at that time. I said, please do it for me, because the neighbor made it seem like she really needed to go. She said, "I'm not going, I will go at six o'clock". She told me they could take her at six o'clock and I agreed that they should take her at six because she wasn't budging. She was very stubborn, wonder where I got that from?

Her neighbor got back on the phone and I told him to just take her at six as she requested, and we hung up the phone. I walked back into the room and Lance ask if everything was ok with Gran Gran. I told him she was ok but, she was refusing to go to the hospital (this was nothing new), this actually happened several times in the last few months. Before the nurse took Lance to the back for surgery, I kissed him, on his lips and we told each other how much we loved each other. We had begun to say it every day. I sat in the surgery waiting area with my aunt, my mother in-love, my mom, and my sister. Surgery lasted around three hours because the doctor had a lot of repairing to do for his left knee. The attendant came out, Humphrey, the lady called. "Lance is out of surgery and the doctor will be out to give you some information". The doctor came out and told us everything went well. He told us Lance was not in a lot of pain due to my asking for a nerve blocker for him. That wasn't offered with the first two surgeries, but I knew to ask for the blocker for this surgery because I had knee surgery before and that is what my doctor gave me. Lance stayed in recovery and was soon moved back to his room. I had a since of peace and we thanked God that surgery was over, and we could finally once and for all move toward recovery. We were settled back into the room and everyone had gone home for the day.

We were both resting after a long day and my phone rang from Texas around six thirty. I couldn't make out what was going on and all I could hear was my Gran Gran's Mexican neighbor saying "Nikki, I put your grandmother in my car at six o'clock to take her to the hospital and once we took off, she slumped over in my car". He told me he called 911 and they were with her in his house. I said ok, "can I speak to her". He said "no, you cannot speak to her because she is not talking". He told a sheriff that I was on the phone and he passed the phone to the sheriff. I asked the sheriff what was going on and if I could speak to my Gran Gran. I had spoken to this sheriff about a month before because my Gran Gran went missing and, I actually found her in the hospital. The sheriff immediately remembered who I was. He said, "Mrs. Humphrey they are working on your grandmother, but she is not responding". I said, "what do you mean, is she breathing". He told me he didn't know but, they were working on her. He told me he had to go because they were getting ready to take her to the hospital, and someone would call me with an update. I started praying, "God please watch out for Gran Gran. I felt so bad because I was not there with her and she was all alone with no family. I loved her and I didn't want anything to happen to her.

I went back into the room where my husband was sleeping, and he woke up just long enough to ask me if everything was good. I told him I thought it was, but they had to take Gran Gran to the hospital. We both fell asleep and when I woke up it was ten thirty p.m. I noticed no one had called me back from Texas. Lance was still a sleep, so I stepped out into the hospital hallway and called the hospital in Texas. I finally got a young man on the phone and explained my Gran Gran was brought there by the squad. I explained I was her only living relative and I needed an update on her status and if they could patch me to her room to speak with her that would be good. He originally told me that he couldn't give me any information over the phone. I said "sir! I'm her only living relative in Ohio and someone needs to tell me something"! The young man told me to hold on. He told me I would need to speak to the head nurse. I said ok and made my way to the visitor's bathroom.

The head nurse got on the phone and said who are you? I told her I was Ms. Ruby's grand daughter and I wanted to speak with her. She paused for a moment and said "mam' I'm so sorry, your grandmother died. I cupped my hand over my mouth and slid down the cold wall in the hallway and screamed inside my hand. My grandma had actually died at her neighbors' home. This was just one more gut punch to the soul of my heart, and it was one more thing to add to my list of traumas. I got up off of the floor and made my way to the hallway bathroom. After I hung up from the nurse, I called my mom crying. She immediately thought something was wrong with Lance until I told her my grandma had died.

She asks if she could come up to the hospital, but it was late, and I knew she was tired. She had been up there with me all day, so I told her to stay home. How was I going to go into the room and keep a straight face? How could I tell Lance Gran Gran died? He loved her just as much as I did, and he had just come out of surgery. I quietly made a few more calls and walked back into the room. He was up waiting on me. He could tell something was wrong by the look on my face. As soon as I walked back into the room, he asks did she die. I shook my head yes as I cried. He began to cry and kept saying "I'm so sorry because I can't even hold you. He was right, he could not hold me. Due to all of his injuries we could barely hug each other. I got back into my blow-up bed and cried into my pillow for the rest of the night. I woke up the next morning with tears in my eyes, my Gran Gran was gone, and we had just gotten started as a family together. I was her only surviving immediate relative and the burden would be on me to fly to Texas and plan a funeral service for her. The thought of me having to leave my husband overnight let alone a whole week was torture. After planning and speaking to the funeral home over the phone I scheduled her funeral service for Wednesday March 6. I had one week before I had to leave my husband. The day came when it was time for me to fly to Texas. Before I left to board my plane to Texas my husband and I prayed and cried because I would be going to Texas by myself to plan an entire funeral service. This would be a whole new experience as I had never done anything like this before. The burden was on me to do it because there was no one else. While in Texas my husband had his first doctor's appointment. They would transfer him from ICU trauma to his doctor's appointment. My mom agreed to go with him, and they would facetime me from the appointment. (thank God for technology and thank God for my mom). Sure, enough when it was time for the appointment my mom face timed me from the doctor's office. I was so happy to see my husband. The doctor told us he was pleased with the progress so far and Lance was doing great with the healing process. Lance's first appointment went great and his surgeon was pleased. I failed to mention not only did Lance have an orthopedic surgeon, he had a kidney doctor, heart specialist, newly added neurologist, speech therapist, and physical therapist. The last four doctors were added because of the three strokes that he had suffered. Every single day Lance was seen by every doctor I mentioned above. Out of all of the doctors that came in the room speech and physical therapy was the hardest to sit through. It was difficult because it was hard to see them challenge his mental capacity with math questions, time telling, and cross word puzzles. Lance was a money, math wizard, he was witty and a quick thinker. To see him struggle with basic task like time while looking at the clock was painful for me to watch. I was nervous every time they tested him on a task because it showed me the effect of the strokes. The stroke happened on the right side of his brain but affected the left side of his brain. I had so many questions. Would this be forever? How would this effect our life? Would I have to quick work?

Well, I did it! It was extremely hard on me emotionally, but I managed to clean my Gran Gran's entire house, disburse the things I did not want and plan her entire funeral. I had visited my Gran Gran in January and at that time we sat down and made a list of everything that she would like to take place in the event of her death. One of the things she requested was that her younger dog T.J return to Ohio to be taken care of by Alexa. Alexa was honored to take on the task of raising T.J. so I inherited a gran dog. Early that morning my sister, my daughter and I got up and got dress and headed for Gran Gran's house one last time. We had to pick up T.J. so he could start his new life. We were told by the vet to give him a little Benadryl in order to keep him calm for the flight. OMG! It was a struggle to get him to stop running from us and take the Benadryl. It was around five a.m. I kept saying T.J we don't have time for this we have a flight to catch. He was not having it, and he kept running from us. We finally caught him and the two of them held T.J and I manage to get a little of the medicine in his mouth. I was hoping it was enough and if it wasn't, he would just have to bark all the way back to Ohio. I'm so thankful my sister and daughter were able to fly down because I was very sad and lonely. They made the trip a whole lot better. We were finally back in Ohio and I went straight to the hospital. As soon as I walked into the hospital room, I rushed to my husband's bed to hug and kiss him. I had missed my husband so much. I showed him the program for Gran Gran's service. It was a good service, but I was truly sad. My Gran Gran was gone, and my dad was gone. Lance seemed to be doing good and sleeping ok. We were grateful because he had not had any more crazy episodes. We spent a few more days in trauma ICU before the doctor came in and said, you guys are moving to a regular floor. We were so excited because we spent a whole two weeks in trauma ICU. Leaving was bittersweet because the nurses on that floor were amazing care takers. I along with my sister and daughter packed up the entire room in a matter of minutes this included my blow-up bed. What I didn't know was they were moving us to the smallest room on the floor. It was literally a match box. The room was so small the hospital bed and my blow-up bed were now laying side by side. It was very small. Did I say the room was small? There was hardly any room for movement. I almost had to climb over my husband's bed to get out of mine. I told the nurse this is not going to work because I lived here with my husband and there was no place to put my suitcase. We stayed in that room one night before they helped us move a few doors down. We settled in that room for a few more days and then the news came. "You are being discharged from the hospital". We were excited to finally leave the hospital. Yes, we were leaving the hospital but, we weren't going home. We had no idea what this would look like, but we figured it was better than being in the hospital. The nurse came into our room and told us that Lance would be transported anytime now so we should pack up our room. Once again, my sister, daughter, and myself packed up the room and loaded things into my car. I decided what would go to rehab and what would go home. We had accumulated so many things while staying at the hospital.

Lance's transportation had finally arrived, so I headed to my car. On my way out of the hospital the receptionist that I had spoken to everyday told me how much she loved the planter I was carrying. She was so surprised when I walked over and gave it to her. Here you go, we have plenty left. "Are you sure"? She asked. "Yes mam' please take it". I gratefully walked through the garage with a big smile on my face. I was glad to be leaving. I got into my car and drove to hospital rehab. I arrived at the large brick building carrying all of our things for our new home. His room would be on the top floor of the rehab facility. His room was located on the top floor all the way in the back to the right. As I walked through the halls, I could tell this was a nice facility, and I was glad about that for my husband's sake. As I got closer to the area of Lance's room, I saw a huge sign before going to through the huge wooden double doors. "BRAIN TRUAMA". I became very concerned as I walked through the large double doors. I said to myself brain trauma, and then I quickly remembered he had suffered three strokes. This entire area was dedicated to those who had suffered strokes and brain injuries. As you walked through the double doors of this floor the doors locked behind you. The only way to get back out of the doors was to be let out by an employee with a key. The doors had to be locked because some patients who had brain injuries could forget where they were and try to escape the hospital. Not only did the doors lock but there was a very loud alarm on the double doors. There was no way for patients to escape unless they wanted to alarm the entire floor. I set up Lance's room and tried to make it as personable as possible before he arrived. After all this would be our new spot for the next four weeks. There was one downside to hospital rehab, I couldn't stay the night with my husband. Lance finally arrived and after the attendant left, I asked how his ride was. He responded, "the ride was horrible. "That man hit every bump he could" Lance said. I immediately started fussing, "wow that makes no sense doesn't he know that you are fragile". "I guess not" he said, and we moved on.

We settled into our new routine quickly and began to learn who the staff was and who we would be working with. The therapist and aides were amazing. Lance and I both didn't particularly care for the nurses that took care of him because they didn't seem as sensitive to our situation. There was an African male nurse that we absolutely loved because he took great care of Lance. One of the first things I did as soon as we got to rehab was set up a code name for Lance. Alexa had given him a small stuffed dog and he got so attached to that stuffed animal. He said the stuffed animal she gave him comforted him because it made him think of our godson and Lance really missed our godson. Lance named the stuffed animal, Milo. I can't even remember where he got that name from but Milo it was. It made since to make Milo Lance's code name and for every person who came to visit him in rehab if they did not say the name Milo, they could not see him. We had to put this in place because my husband was a well, known pastor. We also had a few cases when people popped up unannounced. Some of them we knew and some we didn't know at all. I understood people missed and wanted to see my husband, but he was truly sick a lot of days. I didn't want people to see him in this state and neither did he. At the end of the day, I was just trying to protect the man that they knew before the accident. Many people seemed to not understand this and so I had to deal with attitudes, insensitivity, and drama. It was just one more thing to add to my already overwhelming plate.

Lance was assigned a new doctor, a nurse, a morning aide, a night aide, a speech therapist, a physical therapist, and now an occupational therapist. Physical therapy was to help Lance walk again. Speech therapy was responsible for helping to connect his brain with words, telling time and cognitive challenges. The occupational therapist was there to help Lance learn how to function as a newly disabled person. This was a hard pill to swallow. My husband went from perfectly fine to now being disabled. One morning we were fine and that same evening we were living in a nightmare. He got up that Sunday morning and stood on the pews and that same night he couldn't even sit up without assistance. I recalled the words that I said to Lance just as the paramedics placed him on the stretcher "don't worry, it will be ok". At the very moment that I stated those words I became my husband's full-time caregiver. My role as his shifted in an instant. Hospital rehab was were this became a true reality. At hospital rehab Lance became very dependent on me. He didn't want anyone doing anything for him except me. This was a problem for many reasons and our stay here were some of the darker times. Lance had made it up in his mind that he would cooperate with everything that he was asked to do while he was here because he truly wanted to home. We soon learned that if he had a positive attitude his recovery would be better. The beginning days were hard, frustrating and heart breaking. I had secretly become angry at the lady that hit him, and I had become angry with this whole experience. I became frustrated and upset with some who had become insensitive to our current situation. Here I am dealing with trauma, heartbreak, death, and defeat and people were upset because they couldn't see their pastor, or they didn't like the way I handled things. Imagine that, there was a way I was supposed to handle all of my newfound trauma. It was so disappointing to hear some of the things I heard during this time and I couldn't even share them with my husband because of his current state physically and mentally. I carried all of this insensitive drama alone and tried to remove the insensitive comments and actions of others from my brain. I had way bigger fish to fry at this time in my life. Besides, I was literally fighting for three people, myself, Lance, and Alexa and they were truly the only ones that mattered.

Nights and mornings were the worse at rehab. Nights were bad for Lance because I had to leave him there at night. Most nights I stayed as late as I could to ensure he was as mentally comfortable as he could be before I left. I left between eleven and midnight every night, running to my car each time because I had to park in the back of the facility where it was pitch black. The security guard on duty gave me that look every night like, lady you are on your own. I enjoyed the morning guard much better, he always greeted me with a smile and seemed happy to see me. My routine was the same every night once I got home. I pulled up to make sure the house looked the same before I left. Once it looked the same, I went in and went straight upstairs and got in our bed. One night I pulled up at the house and the garage door was opened. I sat there for about 5 minutes studying the house. Did I leave those lights on, I thought to myself? I knew I had turned those lights off because I never left them on. It was around 11 o'clock at night and my first thought was to call my one sister who lived alone. I called her phone and got no answer. I thought who else can call or should I go back to the hospital. I then thought to myself I can't leave the house like this so going back to the hospital was not an option. I sat there thinking all sorts of crazy things. I finally called another sister and her husband. I felt so bad for calling them at that time of night. I never thought to call my husband because he would just lay there and worry and there was nothing he could do anyway. My sister answered, "hello". I said, "I hate to ask this, but I think someone got into the house and I'm afraid to go in". She immediately said they were on their way. They live about ten minutes from our home, so I didn't have to wait long. I felt horrible calling them, but I felt like I didn't have a choice. They arrived and I told my sister's husband he had to go first (I'm already a big chicken anyway). He went in and walked through the entire house with me checking every area. My sister could tell I was nervous, so she offered for me to stay the night in the butterfly room (a room she created for her granddaughter). I really just wanted my bed although I was terrified. I told her I would be ok after we discovered it had rained in Canal and the power went out which was the cause of the lights being on. I looked around and everything was flashing. We laughed and I apologized once again for bringing them out of their house that late at night. I told them thank you one more time before I let them out. Once they left, I was still very nervous. I went upstairs and got dressed for bed and locked the bedroom door. I took out Janet Jackson (a nine-millimeter Glock). I laid it at the headboard of our bed and said out loud, "if anybody comes in here tonight you won't be leaving alive". I meant every word of what I said.

    I would rise as early as I could to get back to hospital rehab. My husband has always been an early riser so that meant I had to get up early and be back at rehab. My husband informed most of the staff that he did not need any of their help because I would be coming. This meant that when I got there I immediately had to get to work. I would get so frustrated at times when I walked into his room in the morning. Not because the aides hadn't done their job, but because my husband would lay in soiled clothing just about all night long until I arrived. My agitation came from him not getting help while I couldn't be there. I wanted the best care for him, and I couldn't give it to him if I physically were not there. They would say we offered to change him or give him a bath and he would say no thank you, my wife is coming. I would say, "babe they are getting paid to help you, you don't have to suffer like this because I'm not here". He would say "I was just waiting on you". He would wait on me, but it was a lot of pressure because although rare, if I was late, he would have the nerve to get an attitude. (That's Lance Humphrey for you). He had literally turned into my little grown baby. I had to change him (literally), change his bed, help him brush his teeth, and get him dressed for the day. I had basically become the morning and night aide. The aides would say, he didn't want me to help him. I would beg and plead for him to let them do their job and he would simply say I don't want them helping me. I want you to do it. So, for the next four weeks that's exactly what I did. I cared for my husband just as an aide would do. They taught me how to properly change him, clean him and dress him.

It was a struggle on my back, but I did it anyway and I did it with a smile on my face although sometimes I secretly rolled my eyes on the inside (LOL). I was willing to do anything that I could in order for my husband to be comfortable and it was the least I could do for him after all he had been through. Physical therapy at rehab was probably the hardest. This was a true test of physical and mental strength for Lance. Lance had endured a lot but not one time did he complain or question God as to why this was happening to him, and to our family. The physical therapist came into the room and said Lance, we are going to stand you up today. Lance said, "ok let's do it". They loaded him into his new ride the wheelchair, and we went down the hall to where all rehab took place. They placed Lance in this huge contraption and ask was he ready. Lance said yes and they stood him up in the contraption built similar to a space suit looking machine. Lance was able to be placed in a standing position for the first time in weeks. The therapist spent several weeks teaching Lance how to basically get in a standing position. We practiced many days of him just standing up and sitting down in his wheelchair. Next thing on the agenda was teaching Lance how to take a step. This was very exciting; however, I had no idea how difficult and painful this would be for my husband. The walking area was a small walkway with a bar on each side for you to hold your balance. It literally took three people the first time Lance tried to take a step. They practiced by standing him up and sitting him down repeatedly. This went on for a few days before they told him they wanted him to try and take a step. Whenever my husband was going to be faced with a challenging task's I would play worship music in the background as a way to encourage him. I stood there trying to figure out how they were going to make this happen because Lance could only walk on one leg. He could not under any circumstances put weight on his right leg so that meant while he was trying to walk on the left leg that still had a brace on it, someone had to hold the right leg. Grunting and moaning Lance stood up but he sat right back down. They stood him up again and counted one, two, three and with all the strength Lance had he took one step. The look on his face displayed pain, and agony. It brought tears to my eyes to see him suffer like this. Although painful he took a step and when he did everyone around him cheered, way to go Lance! I was so excited and proud of this small accomplishment.

Lance was progressing very well, and he eventually worked his way up to eight steps and also graduated from speech therapy. Lance loved the occupational therapist, but he did not like her assignments because they all involved him becoming more independent and doing things for himself. I told the occupational therapist on him every chance I got. She would say, "Mr. Lance, you have to get in the wheelchair, get to the sink and brush your own teeth". It was so hard going from the bed to the wheelchair but eventually we both learned how to do it with ease. Next task was using the bathroom. The first time I tried to get him to the bathroom by myself was a complete mess. We first had to use the sliding board to get him into the wheelchair from the bed.

Next, we had to get the wheelchair into the small bathroom and get him off the wheelchair and onto the toilet. Not only that I had to find a way to pull his pants down over the brace that could not be removed. I told him let's just wait on the aide, but I knew Lance was going to make me go through with this production because he didn't like to wait for anything. He managed to use the bathroom in the toilet for the first time and we were excited about this accomplishment. It was a challenge, but we didn't care, we got it done, and we did it together. I got Lance back into the wheelchair and then from the wheelchair to the bed using the sliding board. "Whew! Thank you Jesus" I said, out loud, "that was hard". As time went on it became easy to get him to the bathroom and eventually Lance learned to do it all by himself.

Lance was enrolled into a few social classes where he had to participate. He didn't like going but learned it was good for him. He went to yoga and played Badminton from the wheelchair of course. He also played board games with the other patients who were in the facility. It made me sad to see Lance struggle with the smallest challenges. He was confused at times and I knew it was due to the strokes. He would also repeat things a lot and he didn't remember a lot of what he was telling me. It made me so sad to witness my husband like this. It was about three weeks of being in rehab before I could admit to myself the old Lance was gone, and I would have to embrace this new Lance. He had been totally changed from the inside out. He would have moments of complete silence where he did not speak to anyone at all. It was as if he was in the room by himself. I would ask just about every day are you ok? He would look at me and say yes why do you ask. He didn't even realize he was distant. The doctors later explained to me that this was called flat effect. It was due to the stroke. He would just go flat, and he would look very sad, but he wasn't. Flat affect was something me and my daughter had to get used to. We had been through a lot and I had seen a lot and even learned a lot, but I never got use to the flat affect. It was something I just dealt with because I had no other choice.

I could tell they were preparing for us to leave hospital rehab when we got wheelchair and car training. Wheelchair training showed me how to push him in the chair. I learned how to operate the wheelchair and how to park it so that he wouldn't roll off. The scariest part of that process was making sure we could get over curbs without falling. I was able to do it with ease, but it made Lance extremely nervous. The car training showed me how to get him in and out of the car with ease using the sliding board. I had no issues with the sliding board because I had mastered it. The day finally arrived when we woke up and the doctor placed a leave date on the board. We were so happy; we could finally go home. Lance started to decline just a little and the doctor changed his go home date. We would have to stay one more week. Lance was mad! I told him it was for the best and we just had a few more days to go and we would be out of there and at home before we knew it but, going home would be a whole other beast that I was not prepared for.

CHAPTER 7
FINALLY, HOME

They had finally given us an official date to go home, March twenty second. The rehab hospital also gave us a finish date for therapy and that included rigging the bell. Ringing the bell signaled that you had graduated from the rehab hospital and you could now go home. It was a huge accomplishment and Lance had come along way. We both did. I was so excited for the day of ringing the bell. I invited all of our close family and friends. We had food, and cake prepared for the special day. It was a full room when he rang the bell. One of the therapists said, wow, this is the most attended bell ringing ceremony that we have ever seen. We took lots of pictures before and after the event so that we could commemorate the special moment. As we all stood around, they said Lance are you ready? He said yes sir, they told him go ahead and ring the bell. As he rang the bell there were shouts of joy, laughter, and clapping. Of course, we were all crying. This moment was so liberating. It signified that we had been released and could finally go home. We spent the rest of the evening visiting with friends and love ones and Lance seemed so happy. I'm sure his happiness was due to us leaving the next morning. I woke up bright and early that morning and hurried to the rehab hospital. I had a lot of energy and I was very excited. I pulled up to the facility and rushed upstairs to his room. Lance had already gotten dressed for the day. They already had his paperwork prepared and provided us with home instructions. As we headed downstairs everyone gave us their well wishes and told us good luck. We had the biggest smiles on our face. Two of his security from our church met us at rehab because Lance wanted to make one pit stop before going home. I helped them to properly load Lance into the car and then jumped into my car but right before I pulled off, I became physically sick. I became so sick that I had to pull over.

I'm not sure if it was nerves or what. I finally got myself together and arrived at our church. That is the first place Lance wanted to go to before we went home. They rolled him into the sanctuary, and he began to cry. His mother and father both met us at the church along with his administrator. I began to play a worship track to create an atmosphere of worship and thanksgiving. His two friends picked up his wheelchair and lifted him on the altar and turned the chair around as if he was facing his congregation. He sat in his wheelchair and cried. Before I knew it cries of thanksgiving and praise overtook all of us. We were so grateful and thankful for what God had done. God had given us a miracle! They took him down from the pulpit and one of his friends rolled him around the sanctuary, they were taking him on a victory lap. We cried and prayed and thanked God one more time before we headed home.

Just before we pulled up to our home it began to rain. It was cold and rainy but as we pulled up, there was my mother and sister with a huge welcome home sign standing outside. I honestly don't know how I could have navigated many of the day-to-day operations without my sister. She had spent all seventeen days in the hospital with me. I videoed my husband being rolled into our home for the first time since Sunday February 10, 2019. He was overwhelmed with emotion and I was just happy to have him home. Before my husband came home, I had to rearrange our entire house. We had to have a ramp placed out front which I had to physically remove every time we left. I also had to lay it out every time we returned home. My brother in-love was a huge help. He had come over and had broken down all of our furniture so that the hospital bed could be placed in the living room. With the love and support of our family I was able to make a lot of things happen. I could not have imagined going through this without our families. Our church family was a huge support as well. Lance and I both know that apart of the reason he is still here, well outside of God is because of the fervent prayers of our congregation. His friends helped me to settle him in his hospital bed and I took a couple of pictures. We were finally home. Thank God. I set up all of the things my husband would need in order to be comfortable. He could access the TV remote, water bottle, bandages, medicine, wash basin, and much more. Because of his injuries which were still severe at the time, Lance had to sleep in a hospital bed, and I had to sleep upstairs in our bedroom. I don't think this mattered to either one of us because we were home under one roof. Before we left hospital rehab, we were given the option to have a nurse come to our home and take care of Lance's basic daily needs. Lance was not having it. He said, "Nichole, I want you to do it". I called my principal and notified my job that I would not be returning, and I would be out until the end of May. I had recently started a doctoral program with an online University, but I quickly learned there would be no way I could keep up with my studies, and take care of my husband, so I had to quit the program. It was bittersweet because I wanted my doctorate, but my husband needed me more. Therapy sessions were far from over and for the next six weeks physical therapy and occupational therapy came to our home. Things were going good and Lance was doing good with therapy. He learned to sit up and down in his wheelchair in order to strengthen his arms. He learned to build strength using exercise bands that they provided for him. He eventually learned to go up the stairs and after sixty -seven days he was able to take a shower. Helping him to shower for the first time was difficult but we got it done and, he was clean. He still wasn't able to put any weight on his right leg at this time, so we had to literally do everything with his left leg only. Between the two of us we got it done and we would say teamwork pays off.

Lance's physical body was disabled, and I had to often remind Lance that he was in a wheelchair because he tried to do many things on his own. This was challenging for him at times because he really wanted to do things on his own. For the first time ever I seen Lance get upset. While in his wheelchair he was trying to fix a cabinet and he was trying to fix the bottom of the cabinet while in his wheelchair. I already knew he couldn't fix it, but I didn't say a word because I could tell he was having a stressful time and I didn't want to add to the frustration. I sat watching TV and pretended I didn't see him trying to fix the cabinet. The next thing I heard were items being thrown on the floor and yelling. He was upset because he couldn't get down to fix the cabinet. I walked in the kitchen and reminded him of how far he had come and told him he would be able to do those things soon. I would remind him of this often when I could tell he was getting frustrated. I had been documenting every detail of the accident this entire time and I would show Lance pictures and videos of how bad off he was, and then I would say look where you are now. I would tell him to remember when he couldn't get out of the bed. Conversations like this seemed to make him feel better.

Home therapy was finally complete and now it was time for outpatient therapy. Twice a week for the next six weeks he would have to leave the house and go to outpatient therapy sessions. I would load him into the car and take him to therapy about ten minutes from our home.

I had to return to work about three weeks before school was out so my husband's good friend who is also the head of his security team at our church took over the therapy visits for me. Things were finally looking up and we had a routine going. We were managing our lives and we believed the worse was over. Lance graduated from outpatient therapy and I had a small cookout to commemorate another milestone in this journey. We had one more, huge event and that was the return back to church.

CHAPTER 8

HEALING

Excitement was in the air as we woke up Sunday morning. It was the day we had been planning and waiting for, our Pastor was returning to church. I had spent weeks planning out every detail for this day to be perfect for the Pastor's return. Lance's administrator was a huge help in organizing and preparing for this day. We had several meetings at the house, and we were interviewed several times so that we could put together a documentary capturing our entire journey from the beginning of the accident to the end of his last therapy session. We had a huge guest list that was full of both our families and friends, plus all of our church members. Everyone was excited to see their pastor and I was excited for them to see him. No one was more excited than Lance. He had been gone for months and he missed the church so much. He cried every Sunday that he could not be at church. This is how I wanted people to see him, smiling, walking, and waving. I didn't want anyone to see him laid up with tubes not knowing if he was getting ready to take his last breath. No one should want to see their Pastor like that. But as my husband says, there's all kinds of people in the world. I got up two hours early in order to get Lance showered and dressed and then I had to get myself dressed. I loaded the walker, and made sure I had everything that we needed before leaving the house. I didn't want to turn back for anything. As we pulled up to the church he started smiling and we were truly excited.

Security (his friends) met him at the car and helped to get him out and in position to hold on to his walker. Once we got into the church and settled in the back his mother came back to greet us, she was so excited he was in church. Hey Pastor, we were greeted by smiling faces. We decided we would show the documentary first before we went into the sanctuary. My husband was adamant that he did not want to go into the sanctuary in his wheelchair, so he went in with his walker. We had worked to create a documentary with my husband's administrator to show the church a snapshot of the things we had gone through during this horrible ordeal. We were supposed to wait until the documentary was completely over before we entered the sanctuary, but my husband couldn't wait. He was ready to go in, so my daughter and I slowly followed behind him and entered the sanctuary. As he entered the sanctuary, an eruption of shouting, clapping and crying could be heard all over the sanctuary. People even began to dance and run. Our pastor was back into the sanctuary. It was truly a celebration and we were all overwhelmed by the many people who showed up to show us love on this day. The celebration lasted well over hour normal two-hour service. Both my husband and I got up and began to thank everyone who supported us, prayed for us, and who truly hung in there with us during this tragedy. We had so many people to thank. We thanked all of our family and friends, and the pastors who had filled in for our pastor the entire time he was out, and they did it free of charge.

There was truly no way to show our appreciation for what people had done for us. It seemed like thank you was not enough, but it was all we could do. There were many well wishes, and it was such a great feeling being back in church with my husband. Not only were we celebrating his return, but we were celebrating his

Pastoral anniversary. It had been 16 years that we had went to our church as the Pastor and first lady. We were also celebrating our daughter's birthday and we concluded our day with a family meal at a local restaurant. It was a great day for us all and our entire family had not been this happy in a long time. We were thankful to God for bringing us this far.

CHAPTER 9

VICTORY

We finally seemed to be settling into what was our new normal. Our lives seem to be in a peaceful state, and we were living. The hospital bed was gone, the wheelchair was gone, and the ramp to our front porch was now gone. Lance could even walk with a cane at times and seem to be doing phenomenal according to the orthopedic surgeon. In the month of August Lance went back to preaching in fifteen-minute intervals. I did not want him preaching at all. I thought it was too fast and to soon. I was nervous and worried about how he would preach, if the sermon would be structured correctly, would he get mixed up while sitting up there. He suffered three strokes and although it was major it was never visible to most. He felt an obligation to preach because he felt like the people missed their pastor, so he needed to do it. Me and Alexa both were not happy about the decision for him to preach at all. His mom struggled with the decision as well. I would tell him, I know the church loves you, I know they miss you as their pastor but what if something happens to you. They would be sad of course and they would even cry but they would move on and find another pastor. I told him if something happened to him me and Alexa would definitely suffer the most. He would not respond to that he would just continue to preach. After a month or so of preaching he worked his way up to full sermons. As the weeks went by, he continued to get stronger and he started walking better but we both noticed something about the right foot. At a follow up appointment with the surgeon Lance questioned the limp that was now a part of his walk. Lance and I both assumed that as the leg healed, he would eventually return to a normal walk. It was at that appointment that the surgeon told him he would have a permanent limp and he would never have the ability to bend his right foot again. He was permanently disabled. Lance shared this news with me over the phone. I didn't have the opportunity to take him to this appointment because I had to work. Over the phone I listened, and I put on a brave tone, only responding with words like, wow. I asked Lance if he was ok as I often did when we got medical news. He said that he was ok, and it was just something else to add to the list, but he was grateful he could walk. I was grateful to, I was truly grateful but when we hung up the phone, I cried and screamed. I was still dealing with trauma and I mainly suffered in silence a lot of days.

I had finally finished the last three weeks of work and I could resume taking Lance to his appointments. I was doing good, but my anxiety and fear was through the roof. I decided to go see a psychologist. As a person with a degree in psychology I know how important it is to get professional help. I believe in prayer and I also believe in sitting on someone's couch too. At my first session I cried the entire time and at that session I was diagnosed with PTSD, anxiety, and adaptive disorder (whatever that is).

Life seemed to pick up like it was normal again for me. I had been to work, I had been going to church, I was singing again, and right back working in the ministry, but I wasn't ok. Mentally I was still a mess. My aunt would do a mental check in from time to time and ask, "are you ok". I would usually say, "yes I'm good" but I wasn't ok. I also didn't want to put anything on anyone else, so it was easier for me to say I was ok. Going to a psychologist really did help me map out my thoughts and mental space. My phone rang and it was Lance, he told me the heart specialist called him. They told us that the hole in Lance's heart had to be closed and if it was not closed, he could risk having another stroke that could be fatal. We were now facing our fourth surgery. Surgery day came and went and the hole in his heart had been completely closed. This was probably the easiest surgery we had faced. I made Lance pack a bag in case we had to stay the night. He didn't want to because he kept saying he would not stay the night, he hated hospitals. He got his wish and after surgery we got to go home.

Life returned to normal as we knew it, normal but different because neither one of us were the same. I went back to work full time because the summer break was over. Lance was walking only with a cane and preaching every Sunday. The three of us me, him, and Alexa were doing good. Our relationship became more meaningful and we truly vowed to live life as if it was our last day. I am a huge kid at heart and I always had a desire to spend Christmas at Disney. I told Lance after everything that we had been through we could not afford to let life pass us by. This Christmas we decided that we would go to Florida and spend Christmas day at Disney. All I ever wanted to do was see Mickey Mouse on Christmas day. We booked our flight and our hotel, and we left a few days before Christmas heading to Florida. I couldn't wait to leave Ohio; I was so excited. Lance was still using a cane and still struggled with walking at times, so I tried my best to make sure he was comfortable. We woke up Christmas morning to the bright Florida sunshine. We have friends who live there so we went and picked them up and we headed to Disney around seven a.m. Disney was everything I thought it would be. Magical, fun, and exciting. It definitely brought out the kid in me. There was singing and parades and the weather was beautiful. What I did not expect was the large crowd that had shown up on Christmas day. It was thousands of people there. Due to the large crowd, we could not get a wheelchair rental for Lance as we anticipated, this meant he had to walk. I of course was concerned, and I could tell the more we walked the more Lance became agitated. He knew how bad I wanted to be there, so he endured the walking. I tried to get him to stop and take a break, he wouldn't. All I really wanted to do was see Mickey mouse.

We finally found the place were Micky mouse was receiving visitors. As we walked up, I could see another line. I told Lance to sit out front and when it was time, I would call him to get back in line, but he refused. It took us about 45 minutes to get through the line, now that was torture for someone who had legs like Lance. Finally, we reached the curtain and Mickey mouse was standing there waiting on us. I was so happy to see him. I had come all the way from Ohio to see him on Christmas day. I took tons of pictures and Mickey was here, for all my shenanigans. I was not the only one excited to see Mickey. Lance took plenty of pictures as well and seeing Mickey mouse put a smile on his face too. Although Lance was tired, he was happy to see Mickey mouse. After our visit we decided to leave the park. That was good enough for me. All I wanted to do was see Mickey mouse, and I did so I was happy. My focus now was to get Lance back to the hotel so he could rest and rest his legs.

We dropped our friends off to their home and I drove us back to our hotel. We were so tired we grabbed something to eat and went to sleep for the night. The next day I planned a spa day and we decided we would go swimming. I woke up the next morning and went to the spa to get my feet done and afterwards Lance would meet me in the pool area. My appointment was over, and we decided to grab some lunch at the pool restaurant before we went swimming. We ordered our food and ate it while we watched others swim. Once we took care of our bill, we found a nice spot to set up by the pool. I noticed Lance was extremely quiet during lunch, he barely said two words unless I ask him a question. I ask him at least three times, are you ok. He responded with I'm fine, why do you ask. I told him you don't seem fine to me, why are you so quiet. I left well enough alone and jumped in the water. "Hey, are you getting in"? He replied "nope". I couldn't believe it, I said "what do you mean, you love swimming". He said, "I'm not getting in". I swam for about an hour or so and Lance announced he was going up stairs. "Well wait on me" I said. I got out of the pool and we went upstairs. We had dinner reservations at one of the fancy restaurants at the hotel. I always had Lance take me to a fancy dinner when we went out of town.

Dinner reservations were set for six p.m. and in usual Lance fashion he had us there at 5:45. We were seated around six or so and ordered an appetizer. This steak house was really nice. I took all sorts of pictures of the meat selection because they aged all of their meat in salt for forty-eight hours, it was really fancy. I had lamb chops and he had steak. We always ordered that when we went to a nice steak house. After dinner we decided to walk around the hotel for a bit. I told Lance I would be right back because I had to run to the restroom. I was gone for maybe five minutes and when I came back to the area where I left Lance, I saw a man sitting in a wheelchair. He looked like he had on the same shirt that Lance had on. As I got closer, I could see that it was Lance sitting in the wheelchair. I thought I was seeing things. I blinked my eyes as to wish this sight away. He was surrounded by hotel security and paramedics and there was also a stretcher right beside him. When Lance turned around his entire face was bloody, and his glasses were off his face. I panicked! I started screaming and crying at the top of my lungs, what happen to him! The security guard said, "I saw him on camera", he started shaking and he fell. I think he had a seizure". I said what? Lance was looking at me with a dazed confused look and he started asking me why I was crying. He kept saying don't cry, I'm ok. That made me cry even harder because I could tell he was very confused. I kept trying to explain to the paramedics through my tears that Lance almost died a few months back, but I was crying so hard I could barely explain myself. I picked up the phone and called our friends who were meeting us at the hotel to hang out. I could barely get out the words that something had happened to Lance. I was hysterical, shaking and crying. I was confused and I didn't know what was going on. One of the paramedics told me that they had to take him to the hospital. As they placed him on the stretcher, Lance kept telling me he was ok because he could see how distraught I was. The paramedics loaded him in the back of the squad, and they let me ride up front. I silently cried all the way there thinking, not again. I asked what hospital is he going to? I told them please take him to the best hospital in Florida and I didn't care how much it cost. They assured me that they were taking us to the best hospital. Once we got into the ER, they had no rooms available, so Lance had to lay in the hallway. I was so upset about that. I was thinking if you only knew what we have been through you would not make us lay in this hallway. God must have heard my prayers about being in that hallway because a few minutes later they rolled us into a room. The paramedic said Lance's blood pressure was extremely high. I shared that with the attending physician just to make sure she all of the information because the paramedics failed to write that down when they brought him in. I also told her the security guard said it looked like he had a seizure. She assured me that he probably didn't have a seizure because there was no history of it. She said he definitely passed out so he will have to stay the night for test. It was obvious that Lance had cut his eye from the fall and they informed me he would need at least 5 stiches. Lance and I were left in the room just the two of us. He asked, are you ok, I said I don't know, I'm scared. I was in another state and without any family. I stood up beside the bed and said a prayer over Lance. Just as finished praying Lance began to raise his arms and yawn (so I thought) as he turned to raise his arm's he started uncontrollable yelling and his entire body began to shake. He started turning blue and his eyes were rolling in the back of his head. I thought he was dying! I ran out of the room screaming, please somebody help me! Something is wrong with him! Please help! Doctors and nurses flooded the room with machines and oxygen. I ran out of the room and down the hallway (I have no idea where I was running to). I called my mom screaming and crying trying to tell her something was happening, but I didn't know what it was. At this point I was sobbing. "Mommy, I can't do it anymore"! I cried. "I can't take this" "Why is this happening?" "Mommy please help me!" She was trying to be as calm as she could to help me regain control, but I was completely done, and I didn't know if my husband had died. I asked my mom if she could please go to our daughter's house and tell her in person what happened. I knew she wouldn't take it well because she never wanted us to leave at Christmas any way. Just as I expected when my mom shared with her what happened she lost it. I hung up from my mom and just as I began to walk down the hallway my phone rang, and it was my first Lady and my bishop. Talking to the three of them helped me calm myself and right before my Bishop hung up the phone, he prayed for me. I slowly walked back to the room and Lance was back asking me and the nurse what happened, she said you scared the (explicative) out of all of us that's what happened. They had caught the end of what I had witnessed with Lance. Another doctor came in and said you definitely can't go home, and you definitely had a Grandma seizure. A Grandma seizure is the worst kind of seizure a person could have, and Lance had two of them within thirty minutes. Just ask the doctor left out of the room his best friend who lives in Florida arrived. I was so happy to see him because he was the closest person, I had to family, but he was leaving in the morning for Ohio. He stayed and visited with us for about thirty minutes. When it was time for him to leave the hospital, he prayed for the both of us and left.

Finally, a doctor came in to stitch up Lances eye and they asked me to step out while they did it. I stood outside the door to ensure everything was ok. I immediately went back into the caretaker that I had been months ago. No longer a wife at that point but a caretaker just as I would have taken care of Alexa. We were finally put into a room around two a.m. and I was tired. The most they could offer me was a chair to sleep in beside Lance's bed. In the room right beside the bed was a nice window and the best thing about being by that window all night was the Florida view. I was glad about that because I knew I would be up all night, and I was. To top off our night, Lance had a roommate who found out that his sister had just died of a stroke. The roommate was also in the hospital due to a stroke. As we lay in the hospital, we had to endure the strange man crying about his sister the entire night.

I spent my night praying for my husband and his roommate. I also have never prayed so hard to leave a place. I just wanted to go home to Ohio. What started out as an amazing trip turned into a nightmare. Lance had been taken early in the morning for testing and an MRI. The test would determine if we could leave or if we had to stay in Florida. I had everyone praying. The major test came back, and it wasn't as bad as they thought.

A neurologist came in the room that morning and ask us to repeat the events from the previous night. She explained that as a result of the stroke Lance had it left a spot on his brain and just like a volcano it erupted causing the Grandma seizure. She diagnosed him with epilepsy and put him on what she thought was the best medicine. She said he would have to start the medicine immediately in order to avoid another seizure and as soon as we got the prescription, we could leave the hospital. I ask could we get our flight tomorrow morning. She hesitated but then asked how long the flight was. I told her it was two hours. She said as long as it was two hours we could go back to Ohio. I got the prescription and packed up our things. I ordered an uber to take us back to the hotel. Once we returned back to the hotel, I ordered my husband some food and packed up both of our belongings. I called the airport to get wheelchair service and help for the travel back home.

The next morning, I rose early to ensure we would make our early flight on time. It was a struggle to go through security with all of our things. I was used to Lance carrying the bags. Lance had been taken straight to the gate by an attendant while I went through the regular security check. I didn't care about any of that I was just glad to be going home. I finally got to the gate and was so happy that my husband was there just as they promised me. I prayed all the way home that he would not have a seizure on the plane and God answered my prayer. When we arrived in Ohio and before we got to baggage claim there standing at the gate was my husband's two security (friends). Standing beside them was my sister. Once I saw them a rush of emotion came over me. I was so happy to be home. While on the plane my husband told me, he was going to a member's funeral. I told him I would hide his key for eternity if he thought he was leaving that house! I truly meant it! One of his friends said Pastor that is not a good idea and I was not going to take you. My husband finally acknowledged it was a bad idea. Once we got settled in our own home, I put him in bed, and made a few calls. He slept for the next two days, which we were later told was normal for someone who had a Grandma seizure. Sunday was approaching and I asked my husband if he had secured a speaker because if he had not gotten one, I could get someone. I had organized and orchestrated along with one of our faithful ministers all of the preachers that filled in while my husband was out. He told me he was still going to preach on Sunday. I couldn't believe it! I called my friend and minister at our church who normally stood in for my husband and told him that my husband wanted to preach. We both agreed he shouldn't do it but there was no stopping him. We got to the church Sunday morning and I had no desire to be there at all. I was tired, I was frustrated, but mainly I was worried and sad. I didn't want my husband to preach. I kept saying if something happens to you me and Alexa will suffer the most.

He finally shared with me that he needed to preach because he didn't want to lose it and not get it back. He did preach that morning and against what I wanted he did great! God blessed him and he didn't miss a beat. In that moment I was reminded that as long as we trust God, he will keep us in any situation, any pandemic. I titled this chapter victory because after all that we have been through, we are STILL here, and we still have the VICTORY!

CHAPTER 10

WHAT WE SURVIVED

I thought listing the things that we survived would give you a bird's eye view of the things my husband and I suffered. Take a look at the trauma and things we lost.

Sunday February 10, 2019 hit head on
Bed ridden
Two broken ribs
Three cracked ribs
Blood Clots
Three Strokes
Broken elbow
Four Surgeries
Crushed right foot
Two steel rods in right leg
15 Screws in right foot
Two weeks in trauma ICU
Four weeks hospital rehab/Wheelchair bound
Permanent disable
Memory loss
Loss wages
PHD cancelled

Emotional trauma
Death of grandma
Pain and suffering
List here the things that you and your spouse have survived.

_____

_____

_____

_____

_____

_____

_____

_____

_____

_____

_____

_____

After reading this list laundry list of traumas, and I still didn't share everything, you will have to agree that our story goes from tragedy to triumph and victory. Here's a quote from Lance's orthopedic surgeon "Lance is a miracle, and he will have a mighty story to tell, those are the stories we like to tell." The last chapter victory is a true testament that my husband and I are true survivors of Love in a PANDEMIC! Fast forward to 2020. Lance and I have certainly changed since accident. Although he is permanently disabled, and I nearly lost my mind we have changed for the better. We have both learned to love on each other more. We no longer take the time we have with one another for granted. We never bother with wasting time on useless quarrels. Those things don't seem to matter, and most of our disagreements we laugh off. Lance and I have learned to live in the moment and appreciate every moment for what it is because we now understand that time is valuable. Sharing my story with you has been liberating. Being able to tell it in my own way has been therapeutic and has brought forth some of the healing that I needed. This was my story, let me help you survive yours.

CHAPTER 11
THE INTERVIEW

After writing and sharing my story of the events that occurred in our lives in 2019, I became intrigued about what my husband had to say as it related to the after math of his accident and how he felt about it today. I was surprised to actually hear his answer.

Nikki: How have you survived the things that you have been through?

Lance: Literally one day at a time.

Nikki: What do you mean by that?

Lance: There has not been one day since the accident occurred that the accident has not been on my mind. Every time I get out of the bed and feel the pain in my leg it literally comes back. There hasn't been a day since February the 10th that it has not been on my mind. So, it's literally one day at a time.

Nikki: I know you survived one day at a time, but did you pray every day? Did you talk yourself off a ledge?

Lance: All of the above. Praying and trusting God that there has to be a reason behind it. I don't understand it but at the end of the day I trust him.

Nikki: Ok, is that it?

Lance: Yeah. But when I would hear your teacher put on Facebook about her accident, I knew exactly what she was talking about. It's a daily fight and you miss the person that you used to be. Um. You know.

Nikki: So, do you miss the person that you use to be?

Lance: I do! Yeah, I do because now, (long pause) it's like your trapped in a big old ball of anxiety. All the time.

Nikki: So, have you seen any upside or victory or hurdles that you have overcome?

Lance: Not yet. I think that's where my frustration comes in at. I haven't seen any positive with me having to go through this.

Nikki: You haven't seen any positives with having to go through but, when you look back, have you seen um. Have you gotten to a place where now, not that you are over it, but you are mentally not the same space you were as the first week it happened?

Lance: Yeah, I've notice as far as me moving on.

Nikki: That's what I'm getting to because we know it happened and you will live with it the rest of your life because there are reminders that it happened. But have you been able to move forward?

Lance: Yeah, and again that literally goes back to the one day at a time. Literally pushing through each day because when you get up you don't know how your day is going to be. What it's going to consist of. Is it going to be a good day mentally, emotionally, and physically? Or is it you know, is it not going to be a not so good day? Sometimes you might be fine mentally, but not emotionally and physically. Then sometimes you might be fine physically but not emotionally and mentally. It's literally a daily fight.

Nikki: So, you're still surviving the accident? You cannot say you survived it and you're done? You are actually still surviving the accident?

Lance: Even though I don't understand it God I trust you behind it. To me, it just hasn't manifested yet. I think it will be a lot easier once the manifestation takes place. It would be easier because I don't understand why. I liken it to a parent. What kind of parent would I be if I caused something to happen to Alexa where she's in pain every single day of her life? It's like you're the father, why would I do something to her, that would cause pain every single day of her life? That's kind of hard to process.

Lance: Every day I wake up and say God I don't know how today is going to be but please give me a great day not just a good day but a great day. Then I start the day.

Interviewing my husband was a huge eye opener. It had been quite some time since we actually had a real conversation about the accident. Although I am still affected by events from the accident it seems that I have been in a state of mind that lives beyond the accident, and some of the trauma. After hearing his response, I should not have been surprised at all. I know and see the struggle that my husband goes through on a daily basis as it relates to the accident injuries. For example, him still having to crawl up our stairs like a baby or having to go down the stairs one leg at a time (one of the things that breaks my heart). Or him not being able to stand long, and his bones aching to the point that he has to put his braces back on. Pain is a way of life for him. What I learned from his responses is that he still does not have any answers as to why this has happened to him and he is basically living day to day with what has occurred. I know that God will provide what he needs.

ABOUT THE AUTHOR

Lady Nikki Humphrey is the proud wife of Pastor Lance E. Humphrey. She is the proud mother of one daughter Alexa Nichole and she is the first lady of the Mt. Zion Missionary Baptist church where she operates as the minister of music and lead servant of the women's ministry. She is a national gospel recording artist and released her first CD in 2013, entitled Life Saver.

She is an educator working in the public-school system and she loves educating middle school students. She came from poverty but with the help of God and her family she has accomplished many things. Graduating and receiving two bachelors and two master's degrees are one of her greatest accomplishments. Nikki recently started a t-shirt business/clothing boutique, Nik Nak Tshirts. Her love for the women's ministry and the marriage ministry inspired the writing of this first book, and this is her greatest accomplishment by far.

While Nikki is very committed to everything that she puts her mind to, her greatest passion is for her family. Her love for her husband Lance is seen and felt by all who know her. Her heartbeat

Alexa Nichole is the greatest gift that God could have ever given her. She is mostly honored to be the daughter of Elder Janet Kimble Smith who raised her to be a fighter, and her aunt Kim, who taught her how to be a warrior. Thank you both..

This section of the book is dedicated to journaling and working through pandemic situations as a couple. Here are some tools that I used to help me manage my relationship when I found myself in a pandemic situation. It is my prayer and desire that you allow our story to prompt you to make the necessary changes needed so that you ensure survival for your relationships.

"Patience"
IN A PANDEMIC SITUATION HOW DOES YOUR SPOUSE CHALLENGE YOUR PATIENCE?

Love notes

_____

_____

_____

_____

_____

_____

_____

_____

_____

_____

_____

_____

Scripture: 1 Corinthian 13:4 Love is patient, love is kind. It does not envy, it does not boast, it is not proud.

HOW DO YOU HANDLE THE CHALLENGE AS A COUPLE?
Love notes

_____

_____

_____

_____

_____

_____

_____

_____

_____

_____

HOW WILL YOU HANDLE CHALLENGES IN THE FURTURE?
Love notes

_____

_____

_____

_____

LOVE IN A PANDEMIC LOVE NOTES
Affirmation: I AM FILLED WITH LOVE, PATIENCE, AND PEACE
List here the ways you can practice patience:

_____

_____

_____

_____

_____

_____

_____

_____

_____

_____

_____

_____

_____

_____

_____

_____

"Life Balance"

HOW HAVE YOU BALANCED LIFE AS A COUPLE?

_____

_____

_____

_____

_____

_____

_____

_____

_____

_____

Scripture: Psalm 127:2 It is useless for you to work so hard from early morning until late at night, anxiously working for food to eat; for God gives rest to his loved ones.

TEN SIMPLE WAYS TO FIND BALANCE AS A COUPLE:

1. Turn everything off, disconnect for the weekend.
2. Trim the things off your life that don't matter. (people, places, things).
3. Pay attention to your health, and your spouses.
4. Spend time alone together.
5. Treat one another to something special. Not costly but meaningful.
6. Explore the world. Take a trip, walk at a park.
7. Spend intimate time together.
8. Spend time with another couple that have the same goals and values as your relationship.
9. Remember to have FUN in your relationship.
10. Remember your relationship matters. (date night is still important).

Love notes

_____

_____

_____

_____

_____

_____

_____

LOVE IN A PANDEMIC LOVE NOTES
Affirmation: **I WILL SLOW DOWN AND ENJOY LIFE.**
List here the ways you can begin to balance your life:

_____

_____

_____

_____

_____

_____

_____

_____

_____

_____

_____

_____

_____

_____

"Positive Love"

Scripture: Philippians 4:8 And now, dear brothers and sisters, one final thing. Fix your thoughts on what is true, and honorable, and right, ad pure, and lovely, ad admirable. Think about things that are excellent and worthy of praise.

WITH YOUR SPOUSE LIST 8 POSITIVE THINGS YOU EXPERIENCE IN A PANDEMIC SITUATION.

Husband:

1. _____
2. _____
3. _____
4. _____
5. _____
6. _____
7. _____
8. _____

Wife:

1. _____
2. _____
3. _____
4. _____
5. _____
6. _____
7. _____
8. _____

LOVE IN A PANDEMIC LOVE NOTES
Affirmation: OUR MARRIAGE IS DIVINELY PROTECTED. NOTHING CAN SEPARATE US AND WE ARE TOGETHER TILL THE END OF TIME.
List here the ways you will continue to show positivity in your relationship

_____

_____

_____

_____

_____

_____

_____

_____

_____

_____

_____

_____

"Finances" (money maker or money breaker)

HOW DO YOU MANAGE FINANCES IN A PANDEMIC SITUATION?

1. Did your finances grow?_____
2. Did your finances decline? _____
3. What was your management system? _____

Scripture: Philippians 4:19 And my God will meet all your needs according to his glorious riches in Christ Jesus.

Tips to help your finances as a couple:

- Communicate with your spouse about financial matters.
- Have a financial plan that is created by you and your spouse.
- Know where you and your spouse are financially.
- Search out resources and tools that can help you as a couple.

Love notes

_____
_____
_____
_____
_____
_____

LOVE IN A PANDEMIC LOVE NOTES
Affirmation: WE WELCOME ABUNDANCE INTO OUR LIVES DAILY

List here the ways you can manage your finances

_____
_____
_____
_____
_____
_____
_____
_____
_____
_____
_____
_____
_____
_____
_____
_____
_____

"Communication"

It is impossible to share a happy healthy marriage without communication.

What is the most effective way to communicate with your spouse?

1. Argue Constructively
2. Don't expect your spouse to be a mind reader
3. Praise your spouse
4. Resolve arguments one issue at a time
5. Be honest (REALLY HONEST)

WAYS OF COMMUNICATION
STOP WHAT YOUR DOING AND PRACTICE ONE COMMUNICATION STRATEGY

WRITE A LETTER	SEND A TEXT MESSAGE
SEND AN EMAIL	CELL PHONE

Scripture: James 1:19 Know this, my beloved brothers: let every person be quick to hear, slow to speak, slow to anger

LOVE IN A PANDEMIC LOVE NOTES
Affirmation: WE ARE EXCELLENT COMMUNICATORS
List here the ways you plan to communicate with your spouse

_____

_____

_____

_____

_____

_____

_____

_____

_____

_____

_____

_____

_____

_____

_____

_____

_____

"Sex and Intimacy"
(KNOW THE DIFFERENCE)

Who initiates? Him or Her
Who is more spontaneous? Him or Her
Who shows more affection? Him or Her

The question is? Would you like to see a role reversal in these areas? Why or Why Not?
Husband:

_____

_____

_____

_____

_____

Wife:

_____

_____

_____

_____

_____

YEP! Still talking about SEX!
Helpful tips for Sex and Intimacy

Pray about your sex life- We pray about EVERYTHING except our sex life. It seems a bit shocking to mention prayer and sex in the same sentence however, God created the act and he made it to be enjoyable. Why not ask his blessing on your sex life? Make it a matter of prayer especially if this is an area of struggle. Just like other areas in your life, PRAY about it. Watch God make it good!

Keep open communication- Discussing sex with your spouse can be a difficult conversation, however a conversation must be had for a happy healthy sex life. It is important for you to be as honest as you can so that your needs are met sexually.

Show one another physical affection- There is more to sex than just the physical act. Hand holding, cuddling, sweet conversations, are just a few ways to be intimate and show affection towards one another.

Ask questions- Asking questions is a part of teaching one another. It helps you to understand likes and dislikes. This may seem weird but questions before and after can be a game changer.
Example Questions to ask your spouse:
Was it good?
Did you like that?
What turns you on?
Are you willing to try _____?
Questions can be very effective for your sex life as a couple.

When it gets boring – Act out a fantasy that is comfortable for you and your spouse.

YEP! Still talking about SEX!

Redefine date night for your marriage- Date night is different when your dating. It's fun, spontaneous, and surprising. When you get married life moves fast however, date night is still an important part of marriage. It is important to plan a night just for you and your spouse. Commit to that night (no exceptions) and work at creating experiences that will keep the fire burning.

Make a plan for it- Life does get in the way. When you first got together sex was fun, enjoyable, and spontaneous. Now there is children, even grandchildren, work, business, and a whole laundry list of things that prevent us from having sex and intimate times with our spouse. The answer to this is PLANNING, YES PLANNING. Read this statement out loud together:

THERE IS NOTHING WRONG WITH PLANNING SEX. Now that you both agree make a plan (if you need to).

Give it to your spouse as a gift. We give Christmas gifts, birthday gifts, graduation etc. Look at sex as a gift to give to your spouse. You should always seek to please your spouse during sex. This takes away the mental thought of "what will I get out of it?" If you focus on providing a gift to one another it will become more enjoyable for the both of you.

SCRIPTURE: SONG OF SONGS 7:6-12
READ IT

LOVE IN A PANDEMIC LOVE NOTES
Affirmation: WE DESERVE LOVE AND WE GET IT IN ABUNDANCE
List here the ways you plan to increase sex and intimacy

_____

_____

_____

_____

_____

_____

_____

_____

_____

_____

_____

_____

_____

_____

_____

This section is to be used by both spouses at any given time. Feel free to write in this section acknowledging the ways you contributed to your relationship.

Today I took care of our relationship by . . .

_____

_____

_____

_____

_____

Today I took care of our relationship by . . .

_____

_____

_____

_____

_____

Today I took care of our relationship by…

_____

_____

_____

_____

_____

Today I took care of our relationship by…

_____

_____

_____

_____

_____

This section is designated for you to leave love notes, and intimate conversations for your spouse.
I love you because . . .

_____
_____
_____
_____
_____
_____

I love you because…

_____
_____
_____
_____
_____
_____

I love you because . . .

_____
_____
_____
_____
_____
_____

I love you because…

_____
_____
_____
_____
_____
_____

This section is designated for planning. Planning should be done by each spouse. In the planning details note the time and day of the plan so that each spouse is prepared.

Let's plan a _____

Place _____

Date _____

Time _____

Attire _____

Let's plan a _____

Place _____

Date _____

Time _____

Attire _____

Let's plan a _____

Place _____

Date _____

Time _____

Attire _____

Let's plan a _____

Place _____

Date _____

Time _____

Attire _____

Let's plan a _____

Place _____

Date _____

Time _____

Attire _____

Let's plan a _____

Place _____

Date _____

Time _____

Attire _____

Let's plan a _____

Place _____

Date _____

Time _____

Attire _____

Let's plan a _____

Place _____

Date _____

Time _____

Attire _____

Scriptures you can depend on during a pandemic.

James 1:2-4

Matthew 11:28-30

Philippians 4:6-7

1 Corinthian 10:13

Hebrew 2:8

Psalm 23:1-6

Matthew 6:25-34

Hebrew 13:8

2 Corinthian 4:16-18

Ecclesiastes 3:1

Thank You

To all of our family and friends who were apart of this journey.

Our entire church family
Mt. Zion Missionary Baptist Church

Mrs. Shank (Ma Shank) for helping me to edit this book. The wisdom that you have given me throughout my life is priceless and I love you very much.

Contact Information for booking
Email: ladiehumphrey@yahoo.com
Facebook: LadyNikki Humphrey
Instagram: niknak_tshirts

Love in a Pandemic